Cyber Defense Training Systems
The Cyber Defense and Research Initiative, LLC
P.O. Box 86
Leslie, Michigan, 49251 USA
info@cyberdefenseresearch.com

ISBN: 978-0-6151-5578-4

Cyber Defense Training Systems
The Cyber Defense and Research Initiative, LLC

This is the first phase of a multi-part computer and digital forensics training system. This corporate and law enforcement training system consists of a text manual with explanations and descriptions with more than 200 pictures, drawings and diagrams. The text manual is designed to support an accompanying laboratory and exercise manual that contains more than 40 forensic exercises to help prepare students for entry into the profession as a corporate computer examiner. The information presented in this training system is believed accurate at the time of printing while current industry practice is researched and incorporated into this material multiple times per year.

This training system is designed to be used in a lecture / demonstration environment and requires the use of associated case image files. College and University faculty may purchase the accompanying forensic case image files for this training system by sending an e-mail to:

info@cyberdefenseresearch.com

In the subject line put: Instructor Forensics Resources.

You can then enter your contact information in the body of the e-mail and you will be contacted on how to acquire the instructor power points and case image files.

Table of Contents

Learner Level of Preparation

This is a corporate computer forensics and examination training system. It was designed for those with an intermediate level of understanding and experience with PC systems. It is expected that the learner has a working knowledge of both PC hardware and operating systems.

This forensics delivery system was designed to provide both an in-depth instruction in computer forensics and serve as a reference tool for future use. Due to varying environments the learner may or may not have readily available access to component examples such as PC system boards, adapter boards or a variety of storage devices. This information can be obtained by dedicated and effective research and hands-on experience with personal computer systems.

Although the Internet has become the worlds most powerful source of information in the history of the world, the information provided can not be immediately guaranteed as accurate. Consider the various search engines as tools of the trade with each requiring validation.

This text manual has an associated laboratory and exercise manual. Each laboratory session and student exercise has a section titled Report of Student Summary. This section is critical to your understanding of the material. You are to carefully consider the steps in the laboratory session or student exercise and report your learning progress in this area.

One of the most important skills in the field of computer forensics includes that of ability to research while holding to efficiency, accuracy and an understanding of the legal aspects of this field. This corporate training system was designed to help the learner understand, develop and refine these skill areas.

Computer Forensics

The term "computer forensics" can be defined as the preservation, identification, recovery, extraction, analysis, interpretation, reconstruction and documentation of computer data using technological and systematic inspection of the computer system. It is often as much of an art as it is a science.

Computer forensics requires adherence to strict handling and retention policies for handling of electronic devices and evidence. The field of computer forensics is associated with practically any field that uses computers or digital storage devices. It is also used to recover data for the purpose of reconstructing corrupted data files and may involve the supporting of prosecuting criminal activity.

Computer forensics analysis software is unique in that it does not rely on the operating system to locate and recover files. It analyzes bit streams regardless of where or how it is addressed or located on the disk drive or in the acquired disk image. Where the operating system relies on the Master File Table (MFT) or the FAT (File Allocation Table) to locate addressable data, a digital forensic analysis includes the beginning of media until the end of the media, including the unallocated or unmaintained space.

Computer and digital forensic software is unique in the respect that it does not alter or permit writing to the media under analysis. To be recognized in industry and by legal jurisdictions, computer forensics software must:

- Be efficient
- Be accurate
- Be thorough
- Be tested and proven
- Not alter the target environment

Computer Forensics Software

There are basic principles involved with any profession. In the field of computer and digital forensics one of the basic principles is is that the source, or evidence drive must not be altered as a result of any handling, acquisition or analysis of that device. Thus, software that is installed on the media that has files to be recovered is not forensically sound and is not recognized as forensic analysis software. There are many file recovery programs available on the Internet that do not fall under the realms of efficient, thorough, accurate, tested and proven, and does not alter the target environment. Computer and digital forensic acquisition and analysis software should be recognized by other forensic examiners in this profession as reliable and trustworthy.

One of the challenges for a computer and digital forensic examiner is that today's disk drive capacities are increasing at a remarkable rate and the amounts of data contained therein is enormous, even up to hundreds of millions of pages of information.

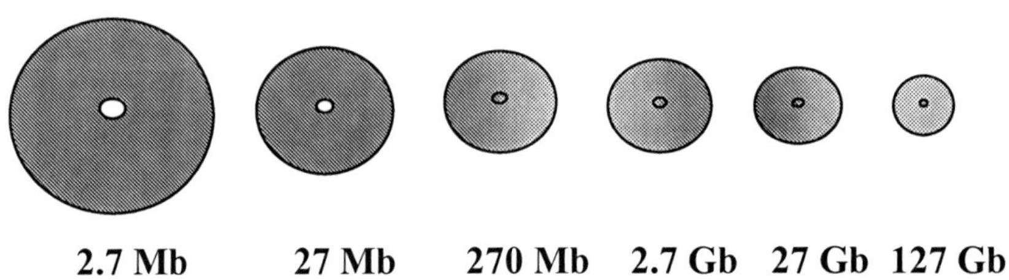

Figure 1

As electronic consumer products become more engrained into our society, the number of storage devices and their capacities increase as well. Today's storage devices include;

Personal Computers	Servers	Lap Tops
RAID	Copy machines	PDA's
Cell Phones	Home Phones	Routers
Switches	Firewalls	Digital Watches
Automobiles	Home Gaming Systems	Thumb Drives

Computer DNA

Human DNA - has remained the same for many thousands of years, however, computer DNA changes all the time. The difference between character encoding and disk data pattern encoding relate to two different concepts. Character encoding represents human readable or other characters in computers and includes encoding methods such as EBCDIC, ASCII and Unicode.

Disk data pattern encoding involves translating of the actual signal transition patterns on the disk. The purpose of this level of data encoding is for the actual electronics to change user data into a pattern of bits that can be stored on the platter. These types of patterns include GCR, RLL, MFM, NRZI among several others. A disk may have any type of signal pattern encoding but still all translate to the same ASCII or Unicode characters.

Magnetic information on a hard disk consists of a data stream of microscopic magnetic fields. These magnetic files contain both a north and a south pole. Thus, data is stored on a magnetic storage device such as a hard or floppy disk b y encoding it into a series of magnetic fields. The determination of the bit being either a 1 or a 0 is dependent upon the read or write polarity of the magnetic field as it passes under the read / write head. For example, as the disk spins and the fields read by the disk read / write head appear as this pattern,

N-S S-N N-S N-S N-S N-S N-S S-N

Figure 2

This pattern might be interpreted as;

0 1 0 0 | 0 0 0 1

Figure 3

Break this byte into two nibbles, and the character encoding would result in a hexadecimal 41. In the ASCII character encoding method an ASCII 41 is equivalent to the capital letter A.

Moore's Law and How it Relates to Computer Forensics

In 1965, the co-founder of Intel, Mr. Gordon Moore, made the prediction that the number of transistors per square inch on integrated circuits would continue to double for the foreseeable future. This prediction has held close since 1965. The result of these technological advances has resulted in the doubling of data density approximately every 18 months. In terms of software, this equates to an increase of 1-bit every 18-months. In terms of forensics analysis, this equates to one order of magnitude every 18-months. When applied to encryption, this is significant in the respect that it can add years to the process of decryption by brute force. Recovering an eight character password is significantly different regarding time requirements than recovering a nine character password.

Which means that no one single individual can recover, review, read and report all of the data available on a single 120 GB disk drive in any realistic amount of time. Thus, an efficient computer forensic examiner must be highly skilled in not only how to use computer forensic software and tools, they must be highly skilled and experienced in investigative methods and procedures to where they become almost intuitive.

Technical Competency

Digital forensic acquisition and analysis involves much more than becoming a proficient mouse "click master". Technical competency involves understanding how the technology works, what it can do, what it can not do, and how to navigate through it when traditional tools of the trade fail to provide access or insight into unique situations". Thus, the necessary technical skills a computer or digital forensics examiner must include command lines, understanding how to decode ASCII, EBCDIC and UNICODE, the binary, octal and hexadecimal numbering systems, how to view and read file and format structures. Additionally, how the hardware, software and firmware interacts is necessary.

Additionally, forensic examiners must have a working knowledge of how to recover deleted data, how to search and analyze recovered data, how to reconstruct deleted, lost and fragmented data, how to use search parameters and how to use various forensic analysis and recovery software.

On the handling side of forensics, examiners must be skilled in and have strict adherence to proper evidence handling and chain-of-custody reporting. They must know how to secure an environment and adequately and efficiently document and report their findings, all with an understanding of associated laws.

Forensic Reporting

Forensic recovery is of little use if the results are not adequately provided or communicated effectively. Perhaps the most tedious aspect of the entire forensic examination process, proper reporting is the documented deliverable of the case. Without it, payments are rarely provided.

COMPUTER FORENSICS INVESTIGATION

CASE 1/11/05-001

DATE
January 11, 2005

Investigator
D. B. Cooper
CISSP, CCE, A+

THIS DOCUMENT IS FOR INTERNAL USE ONLY. ALL INFORMATION CONTAINED WITHIN IS CONSIDERED CONFIDENTIAL

Figure 4

The forensic report should be excruciatingly detailed and comprehensible to both technical and non-technical personnel. This is perhaps one of the true arts of this profession. The other involving the developing of intuitiveness in analysis and examination of the particular types of media and fine tuning ones skills in locating hidden or lost data.

The Forensic Examiners Most Important Software Tools

Forensics software must be maintained, recorded, licensed and legal, else the integrity of the forensic examiner and that of the forensic examination is compromised. The computer forensic examiner needs software that is provides the following services:

1. Forensic imaging and acquisition software
2. Forensic analysis software
3. Search engines
4. File viewing tools
5. Hex editing tools
6. Format viewing tools
7. Disk analysis tools

The Forensic Examiners Most Important Hardware Tools

Like software, forensics hardware must be maintained, recorded, licensed and legal, else the integrity of the forensic examiner and that of the forensic examination is compromised. The computer forensic examiner needs the following hardware:

1. A complete forensic system that can process any type of format.
2. A write blocker
3. An evidence storage system
4. Pertinent policies
5. Logs of work done and evidence handling
6. A digital camera.
7. Computer tool kit
8. Electro-static discharge equipment
9. DOS boot disks
10. Flash card readers
11. Diagnostic software
12. Policies for sanitizing media, verifying integrity of the hardware, storage of media and chain of custody
13. Source hard disk
14. Working hard disk
15. Practice systems

Time Sensitive Information

Being that computer systems contain much volatile information in RAM, the forensic examiner "may" need to recover this volatile information prior to directing their attention towards the issue of the hard disk or other media storage devices. Generally, law enforcement considers this an unwise practice and in most cases it is, however, there may be times when the volatile information that is contained in RAM may need to be captured. In the case of possible use of a computer during a suspected terrorism situation. The system connection and running program information may be as vital as the information located on the media. Removing the power from the system will result in the loss of knowing what that system was connected to at that moment in time and previous connections during that systems power on state. The examiner may need to learn the following on-site prior to removing power from the system:

- State of the System addressing information (ipconfig /all)
- Identify the OS, SP, (may be a virtual environment)
- System date and time
- System uptime (srvinfo)
- Drives and shares (local and network)

Information the Examiner May Need to Learn Back in the Lab

Once volatile information has either been acquired or determined it was not needed for this acquisition, the forensic examiner can create an image of the original media and analyze it for desired data or information. Some of the information the examiner may need to learn during the actual hands-on analysis phase may include;

- Does malware exist on the system
- Are there trojans or viruses on the system
- What the system was being used for
- The recovery of all data, current, deleted, partially overwritten, lost, hidden or secured.

The Forensic Process

- Must not modify or contaminate the media or data
- Must acquire the image
- Must authenticate the data
- Analysis of the data, to include
  - Documentation
  - Worksheet
  - Chain of Custody
  - Preservation
  - Identification

Understanding Hardware and Operating System Interaction

Forensics examiners can not work in a box and must understand what happens when an event is processed by the computer system. The difference between a boot and a post is critical to understand. POST is an acronym for Power On Self Test and does not involve the operating system. All actions that take place during the post are the result of the microprocessor executing self test instructions stored in the system BIOS (Basic Input Output System).

The boot process initiates after a successful POST operation. Even something as common as booting or shutting down the system will alter the evidence or target drive. In fact, just booting the Windows XP operating system will:

A. Will write a recycle bin to the drive
B. Will change and overwrite disk space

Normal shutdown of a Windows Operating System or applications will perform the following actions on the hard disk:

A. It will write files to the disk as part of a close-out process
B. Closing the browser will save any open cookies
C. Closing text editing programs will write to the hard disk

Thus, the importance and significance of the forensic device known as a write blocker is required prior to accessing any source forensics device.

Remnants and Artifacts

To put the subject of computer forensics into more of a perspective, consider the creation of a simple text file. How many pieces of data are created just to create a single .doc file?

This is a text file. Look at how many files are created just to create this simple doc file!

Figure 5

Some text editors create multiple remnants of the original document. This is due to several factors, including built in safety features that will auto save a file during its construction. Additionally, when a file is printed across a network it is copied to something known as a print spool on a print server. Additionally, the operating system Swap file is utilized during memory paging operations.

These artefacts are the result of the software application and not related to any hardware technology. Considering use of a personal computer to surf the Internet yields much more information stored on a disk drive.

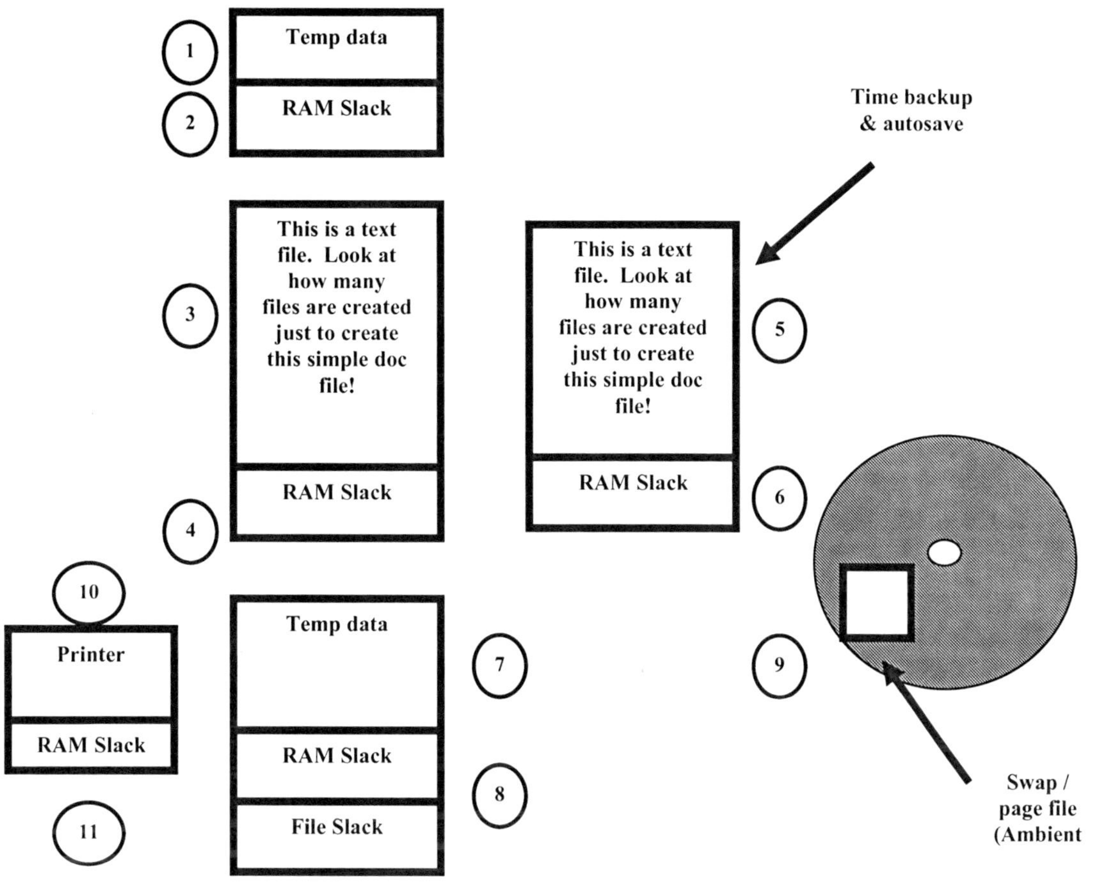

Figure 6

This is a significant amount of additional data and in a forensics examination can be as revealing as the original document. When media is analyzed, it is not just the source document that is desired but this artefact information as well.

What Computers Do

Computer technology involves the processing and storage of electrical impulses. These impulses are discrete and categorized as binary strings. These individual pulses are known as bits and when combined with other pulses comprise a hierarchy of data and information.

Eight bits is known as one byte. Four bits is known as a nibble. Older hard drives had capacities in the megabyte range. Hard disk drives of today range from 100 to several hundred gigabytes. One megabyte is equivalent to one million bytes, or, one million eight bit groupings. One gigabyte is equivalent to one billion bytes of information. To put this into perspective, this entire book consists of less than two megabytes of digital storage.

At their lowest level, for example, a string of electrical pulses in the sequence, off, on, off, off, off, off, off, on, would be interpreted as a binary 01000001. This binary data pattern would be interpreted as the capital letter A. The binary data string 01000010 is equivalent to the capital letter B. The binary string 01000011 is equivalent to the capital letter C. Combine all three of these binary strings together and send them across the Internet to another computer, and the letters ABC might appear on someone else's computer screen.

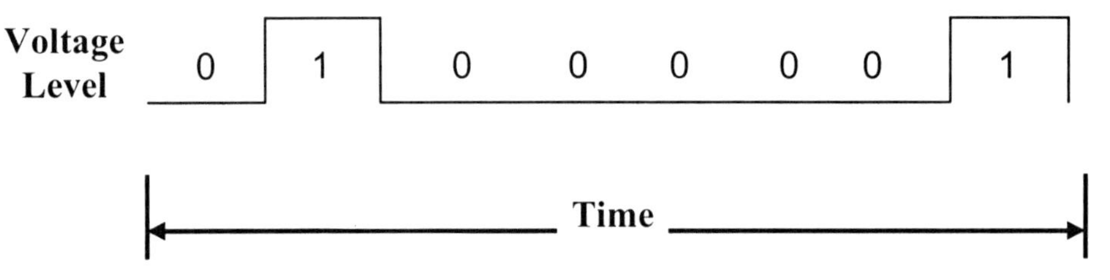

If interpreted as data, this binary string would represent the capital letter "A".

Figure 7

Combine sequences of predefined binary data strings and entire words and messages can be stored and transmitted. For example, the word Hello is comprised of

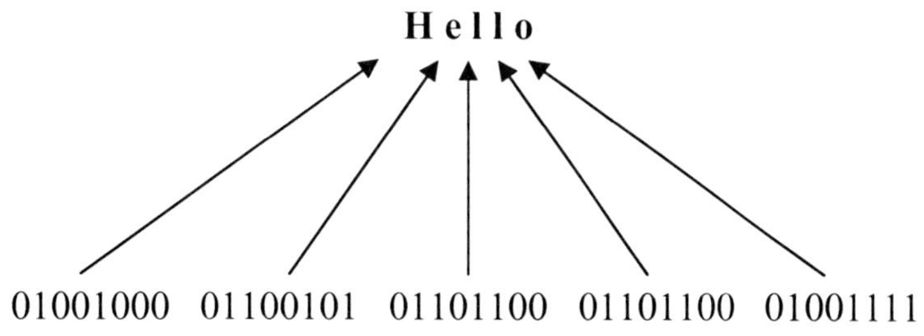

Figure 8

Where the capital letter "H" is equivalent to the binary sting 01001000, the lower case letter "e" is 01100101, and so forth. The amazing aspect of this very simple concept is the speed at which it is performed and the great distances that these data patterns transverse. A kind of 19th century electronic morse code.

As stated previously, a computer is not a television, it is a portal into cyber space where the user dictates what it wants to the computer to do. The computer stores the input in binary while the operating system keeps track of where it is and how to process the data. The hardware does the work of the operating system.

The significance of this concept of a data stream is that, even if the operating system does not keep track of the data stream, (deleted data), it is still on the drive, unless overwritten by a subsequent data write operation. What makes a forensic examination of a computer disk so revealing is that a forensic examination of a disk drive does not rely on the operating system to locate and present the lost or deleted data.

Effective forensics software will acquire ALL binary data steams for analysis. So, if someone deletes a file, you can get it back very easily. If a bad guy tries to hide a file, you can get it back without relying on the operating system to do so. The concern at this point is to make sure the data streams contained on the drive are not altered, thus, proper evidence handling of electronic devices is critical.

As previously stated, computer systems are very revealing. This is due to the fact that a disk drive was designed to store information, not delete or erase it. Today's disk drive capacities are increasing at a remarkable rate where the amounts of data contained therein is enormous, even up to hundreds of millions of pages of information on a single computer disk. The challenge for law enforcement forensic analysis is sorting through all of those these files, including the operating system files.

The number of devices that contain electronic data storage increase daily. Not only personal computers and lap tops, but copy machines PDA's, cell phones, home phones, computer printers and home gaming systems. The race to keep up is, well, like a knowledge treadmill. But what they all have in common is the data is stored as binary strings. If the string can be recovered, it can be analyzed. It may be encrypted, fragmented or partially overwritten, but it still can be analyzed.

When a user interacts with the operating system of a computer, they are issuing commands to it. Even something as simple as clicking a mouse will initialize a sequence of instructions to be performed. This is done in layers of translation and software responsibility. The GUI, or Graphical User Interface, interacts with the human and the higher layers of the operating system. The lower layers organize, track, assign and maintain the data by issuing predefined commands to the computer chips, also known as the hardware. The hardware, through the miracle of physics, stores the information on what ever medium the user defines, usually a hard disk, and the information on the hard disk stays there until it is overwritten.

The GUI in itself is nothing more than picture software that interfaces with the user so commands can be presented to underlying layers of the operating system. The interest in the GUI rests with how the user configured the GUI and with what programs. All of the programs that the user installed via the GUI is recorded in something known as the Registry.

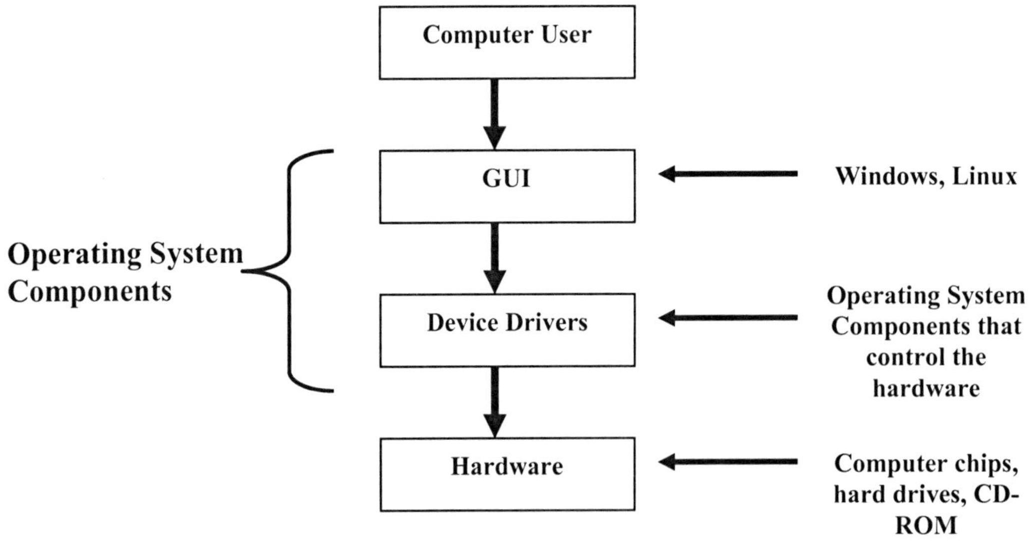

Figure 9

Although a very simplistic view of a very complex operating system, the point is that the native operating system device drivers are generally not the focus of a forensics examination and are often eliminated from analysis. Each of these files has a fingerprint like signature known as a hash value. Since the majority of operating system files do not change, these fingerprint hash values are stored in a database and compared against the hash values of those from the evidence drive. If the device driver or other operating system file has not been modified, this hash value does not change and the file may be eliminated from analysis. If even a single character is modified, the hash value changes and it can be included in the analysis.

If the system is active, meaning, currently operational, RAM, or Random Access Memory, tells the current state of affairs. The programs that are running, the IP address of the computer, what systems this computer has connected to, and much more, is loaded into RAM. Thus, when seizing a computer the decision must be made, do I want the contents of RAM included with this case. If the answer is yes, then simply pulling the plug, as is done to freeze the state of the hard drive, is delayed. RAM contains volatile information, meaning, if the power is removed from the system it will be lost forever. Most criminal situations would not require this information, however, some situations do. A batch file recovery program is provided in Appendix A at the end of this book. This will permit the capture of such volatile information prior to pulling the plug.

This is contrary to how we traditionally shut down a computer but is necessary in order to preserve the information on the drive. To preserve the state of the hard disk, the system should never be permitted to sequence down to a shut down state. Most operating systems, including Windows, write files to the disk when shut down. Doing this on a computer that may be the subject of a forensics examination may potentially overwrite data of evidentiary value. This is why the power is removed instead of shutting down the system. What is on the drive at the time the plug was pulled, stays on the drive. Additionally, some people install cyber scrubbing programs that will begin to overwrite selected files in the event a specific "hot key" or designated key on the keyboard is not depressed during the shut down process. In effect, pulling the power from the system has the effect of freezing the cyber state of the system, with the exception of the contents of RAM.

Hard disk technology is the focus of many forensics examinations because what is on the drive is sometimes difficult to remove by the user. Although an experienced computer user can easily sanitize their hard drive from unwanted or sensitive information, most people either do not know how or simply do not do it. And what is on the computer may not have been put there intentionally by the user. The operating system, in a virtual sense, has a mind of its own. It periodically saves information and it does so in consistent sizes, or predefined blocks of data.

Consider the writing of this book. A text file is opened using the Microsoft Word application. An area of RAM is mapped and reserved for the application program and the data that will be generated by the user. As I create text for my book, I am creating a variable amount of information. This information must fit into container sized sections of the hard disk known as clusters. Each cluster consists of a specific number of smaller containers known as sectors.

If the file I create only fills up three sectors, and the disk drive uses cluster sizes that require four sectors, the operating system will write three sectors of my file and one sector of RAM slack, for a total of four sectors. When I go to save my file, I do not only save the text that I have created, but what ever is in RAM next to that file as well. This is one way the bad guys get caught! The remnants of a previous visit to a web page, downloaded e-mail, or some other aspect of cyberspace, may be written to the disk drive as well.

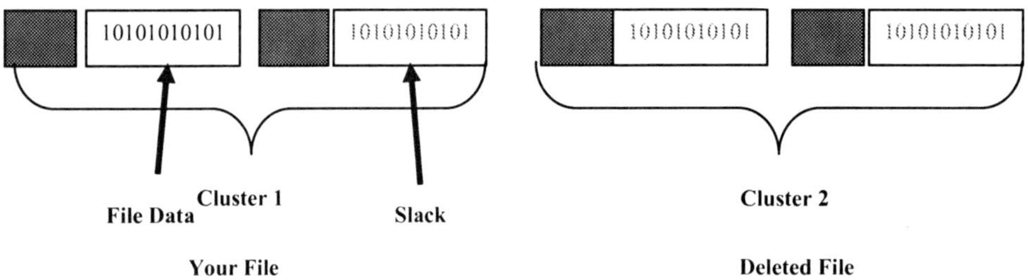

Figure 10

The above example indicates the file you created consists of one sector of data. The operating system writes to the disk in cluster sizes consisting of two sectors. Thus, when you save the file, the operating system take the information you create and assigns it to a cluster, along with residual RAM information to make a consistent cluster size. Only the operating system knows that the first sector is your data.

The reason for this is purely technical. Information is saved much like putting papers in a container, instead of the individual pages of a book. If a container will hold 50 pages and you only create 45 pages, an additional five pages of RAM will be included as part of the operating system write operation. This additional information, is RAM slack and contains contents of RAM that are left over from previous operations. So, if someone were to ask the question, how does information get on the disk even if the user did not put it there, and where did it come from, the answer would be, the operating system put it there and it came from left over portions of RAM.

The Personal Computer Market

The issues surrounding the introduction of the first commercial personal computers involve the goal of mass producing them. Security was not the objective of the first PC's and we have evolved from that platform to slightly more secure operating system characteristics. It should be noted that the personal computer was designed for convenience, not security. Secure computer systems cost many times the amount and some are designed specifically for military or other government operations.

The reason a computer stores and may reveal much sensitive information is the result of four factors.

1. A personal computer was not designed to be secure. It was designed to be mass produced. The underlying technology behind mass produced personal computers is for convenience, not security.

2. Web surfing is generally stateless, meaning, a visit to a web site only involves capturing the image, much like a taking a "snapshot". The visit to the web site is not a continuous connection. If it were, there would be a drastically limited number of web surfers that could visit that site. This snapshot is stored in RAM and / or in the Temp folder located on the hard disk. Any additional navigating through the actual web site entails taking a quick snapshot of the subsequent web pages. These web site captures are stored in the Windows Temp folder and are easily recoverable from the hard disk.

3. Disk drives are designed to store information, not erase it. If they were, they would have an independent erase head built in. This erase head would have a wider write width than the information write head. Instead, disk drives are erased by using the same read / write head. Thus, the aspect of shadow data is inherent in most disk drive technologies.

4. Society has become dependent upon computing technology and cyberspace before it was designed to be secure. Current measures and products are aimed at securing this technology, however, it is far from off the shelf concept of the CIA triad, that of maintaining Confidentiality, Integrity and Availability.

Computers are not Inherently Secure Because

1. Encryption is an option
2. Disk drives, CD-ROMs and tape media, were all designed to store data, not erase it.
3. Common platforms link hundreds of millions of users
4. When you are connected to the Internet, you are connected to the \ entire world of cyber space
5. When you are connected to the Internet, the entire world of cyber space is connected to you
6. The original intent of a computer system, by need and design, was to store and process data.
7. The explosive PC market emerged as the result of a highly fertile business and educational environment, cultured by the insatiable appetite of an open market in business and entertainment.
8. Security is expensive. (Although a security breach can be much more Expensive)

Thus, until systems are designed and manufactured as inherently secure, alternative steps must be taken to mitigate the numerous vulnerabilities and threats against the confidentiality, integrity and availability of our nations number one product, *Information.*

Where Computer Forensics Fits In

As stated previously computer and digital forensics involves the preservation, identification, recovery, extraction, analysis, interpretation, reconstruction and documentation of computer data. It may also include identifying the history of data and / or information stored on the storage device and any and all activities associated with the storage of data on the device, without altering any of the environment.

The most fundamental piece of computer forensics hardware is the write blocker. The purpose of a write is to maintaining the integrity of the frozen state of the system. Alteration of the environment while in the custody of either the corporate examiner or law enforcement does not provide a healthy situation for either situation. A forensic write blocking device will allow data to pass from the drive but not back to it. Thus, recovery of data is possible without altering the original environment.

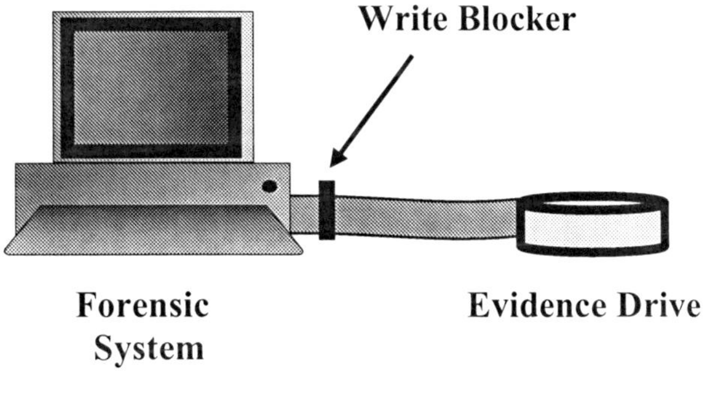

Figure 11

The purpose of a write blocker in a forensics examination is vital to maintaining the integrity of the frozen state of the system. Remember, alteration of the environment while in the custody of law enforcement does not provide a healthy situation for the prosecution. If a disk drive is installed into an examination system without preventing any possible write back operation to that drive, the Windows operating system will write files to that device, thus, overwriting potential evidence. A forensic write blocking device will allow data to pass from the drive but not back to it. Thus, recovery of data is possible without altering the original environment.

With a write blocker, data can be read from the drive but now written back to it. This provides the assurance that the data was recovered without altering the original. To validate this, a hash value (digital fingerprint) of the drive is created during the image acquisition and compared to a hash value created for the copied image. Correlation validates that not one single bit of data has been altered or lost during acquisition of the data.

Forensic Analysis Includes

When we consider the aspects of computer technology and the possible phases of recovery, we appear to learn a new language. Computer and digital forensics involves almost every aspect of technology. The learner of computer and digital forensics is dealing with a cross pollination of technology and society. All professions now utilize computer technology.

File Extensions Keywords File Compression Non-Repudiation
Temporary Folders Volatile Memory CD-ROM's
Logic Bombs Tape Drives Confidentiality
RAM Slack System Services
Integrity Log Files
Policies Applications Objects Hash Values Availability
Encryption Temporary Files
Viruses Sniffing Disk Drives File Slack
Event Viewer Configuration Files

Forensic Analysis

Registry Settings E-mail Messages
Administration Tools Applications File Permissions ASCII
Processes
File Signatures Unicode Malware Physical Security
Unallocated Space Time Stamping
Access Control Methodologies Swap Files
Boot Sector Deleted Files Folders Personnel EBCDIC
Operational Security
Worms Access Times
Print Spool Hacker Tools Backup Systems Auditing

Identifying Hardware Old and New

It is vital that the computer examiner have adequate hardware, application and operating system skills. Computer forensics is not a point-and-click profession. It involves the removal, handling, insertion and storage of media devices as well as motherboards, video adapter cards, network cards, sound cards and a range of other devices. Technical competency involves much more than computer literacy. Technical competency requires comprehension of each component and how it interacts with the rest of the system.

It is important to realize that the physical interfaces between computer components have strict tolerances with both voltage and current. Additionally they have specific timing rates and bandwidth capabilities and are not interchangeable in most cases. A floppy connection will not accommodate a USB device. An IDE hard disk drive will not accommodate a SATA connection.

The number of pins is something that a forensic examiner must be familiar with as it is one method of identifying what type of cable it is. For example:

Floppy interface cable: 34 pins
IDE interface cable: 40 pins (39 actual with one missing)
SCSI interface cable: 50 or 68 pins

Some IDE cables are referred to as 80 pin cables. This is not correct. There are 80-pin wires but still only 40 pin connections.

The hardware aspect of this material, including various terms and concepts are to be addressed in the laboratory and exercise manual. You should complete these terms as part of your first exercise.

Perform Forensics Lab # 1

TITLE: System Component Identification:

OBJECTIVE:

To identify computer system components to include, system motherboards, disk drives, peripheral interfaces, adapter boards, IDE, Floppy, SCSI, parallel, serial, USB, monitor, keyboard and other connections.

Perform Forensics Lab # 2

TITLE: Understanding, Configuring, Recovering and Saving CMOS Settings

OBJECTIVE:

The forensics examiner will learn how to recover and store CMOS setting information.

Beginning Steps in Computer Forensics

To maintain 100% integrity in the acquisition and analysis of a digital image, some basic principles for this profession must be adhered to. First, the state of the system must be froze, that is, not allowed to change during or after the acquisition process.

Freeze the state of the system!

The examiner must not do not do anything that will alter the source device data. This includes **NOT**;

- Shutting down the system
- Installing software
- Uninstalling software
- Leaving the system or media accessible to others who may inadvertently use the device

The Goals and Steps of a Forensic Analysis

Frequently involves the interviewing and documenting of individuals. This can be accomplished by:

- Setting priority of interview process
    - What is the objective of the interview process?
    - What type of questions will you ask regarding system use or access
    - What types of files will you be interested in recovering or analyzing
- If working with attorneys, it is important that you get a memorandum of understanding as to the scope of the project
    - What time frames are you facing regarding recovery of the files
    - What is the financial rate for your services

- Photograph (do not video tape) the system and environment if necessary. This is typically not performed in a simple file recovery situation. You should photograph:

  - The front of the system
  - The back of the system

If the examiner is using digital pictures the authenticity of the Pictures may be questioned. Some examiners have advocated the hashing of the picture when acquired from the camera. Some feel this provides an added level of assurance while some feel this is an unnecessary step.

Unknown Autorun Features

Consider inserting a CD-ROM disk into your $10,000 forensic analysis system only to have an auto run file from the CD begin to erase your operating system. This has been known to happen and is an effective technique in training future forensic examiners to not trust unknown media.

To disable the autorun function on a CD-ROM, hold down the shift key while the CD-ROM disk is spinning up. This will disable the auto run feature which may initialize destructive activities. The CD-ROM can then be analyzed.

Pulling the Plug

When seizing a computer system for analysis, its state of operation is vital and must be considered. If the system is operational, the power cord to the system should be unplugged. It should be unplugged at the system, not at the wall. This will create a time line of events that is part of a controlled environment.

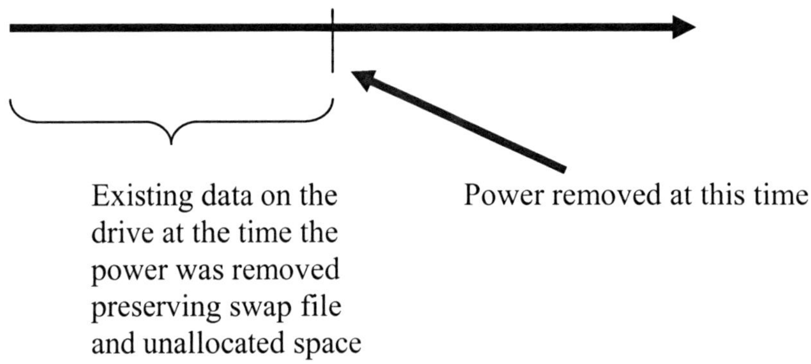

Figure 12

Thus, no changes to the drive, files or unallocated space is possible after the point in time the power is removed. The state of the hard disk and other media is frozen. The disadvantage of this step is that the system will lose unsaved data. Additionally, the state of the swap file is maintained.

This is generally the best step for an individual workstation. However, not all systems are this easy. There are multiple types of systems with multiple types of services they are providing. Database servers contain much information and pulling the plug may affect multiple other users. Never pull the plug on a computer system without proper authorization to do so. In most cases, you should not be the one to pull the plug. This should be the responsibility of the network personnel assigned to maintain the system or server.

Example of a RAID System

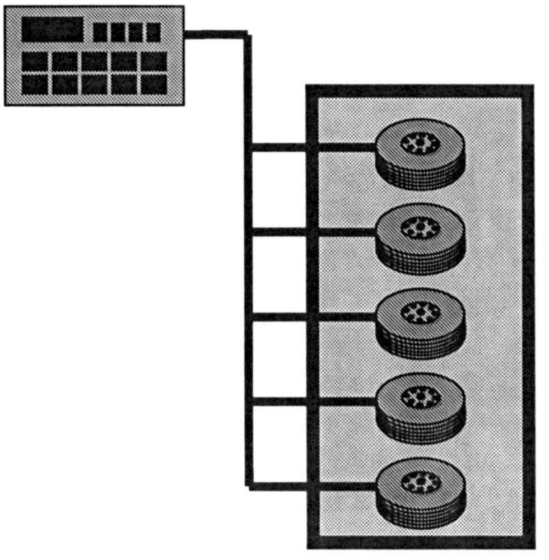

Figure 13

RAID systems are highly dynamic and may require a real-time recovery where the examiner may have 30 minutes or less to perform the recovery. RAID is an acronym for Redundant Array of Independent Disks, (also referred to as Inexpensive Disks). RAID systems stripe or parallel data across multiple platters and disks and recovery here is difficult and challenging. It is recommended that specialized and direct hands-on training be provided for RAID systems before attempting such a recovery. Pulling the plug on a RAID system may or may not be the appropriate step and this decision must be made on a case by case basis. This program is not designed for RAID systems.

SWAP Files

The Windows operating system uses a "scratch pad" approach to optimizing the use of RAM. This scratch file is known as a swap file and is used to "swap" data and files between memory and the hard disk. This provides a virtual memory concept and can contain from hundreds of megabytes of information up to gigabytes of information.

Swap file names per operating system:

Windows 95 (WIN386.SWP)	Windows 98 (WIN386.SWP)	Windows ME (WIN386.SWP)
Windows NT 4 (PAGEFILE.SYS)	Windows 2000 (PAGEFILE.SYS)	Windows XP (PAGEFILE.SYS)

Swap files may be dynamic or static. A dynamic swap file will be cleared upon normal system shutdown. A static swap file will be a defined file and the size is determined by the use.

A Forensic Analysis Must Include

The forensic analysis of a particular media is not limited to analyzing the media using software. Many steps are involved and require the following:

- Protection of the evidence
- Proper evidence handling
- Forensic analysis of the media
- Confidential reporting of the findings

EVIDENCE HANDLING AND PROTECTION OF EQUIPMENT

This involves being aware and cautious of the sensitivity of electronic devices. Electronic circuit boards are susceptible to events known as electro-static discharge. To demonstrate the significance of and ESD event, consider walking across the carpet and touching a door handle or shaking hands with someone. The shock felt and the "zap" sound heard is the result of an electro-static discharge. Static electricity builds up and when it finds a path that it can overcome, it takes it. The issue here is that this small electric shock you felt and heard was in actually several thousand volts. The reason it did not kill you was because it did not have enough current, or electron flow behind it. Although it only made you jump, this voltage will destroy microelectronic circuits.

To mitigate the possibility of and ESD event damaging or destroying your electronic evidence, anti-static bags are used to protect the drive. These anti-static bags actually are conductive, thus, no static voltage potential can build up.

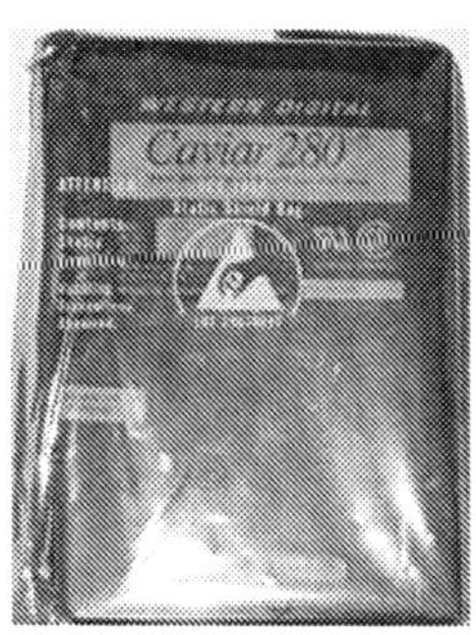

Perhaps one of the best guidelines for handling of electronic devices for forensic examiners is found in the document, U.S. Secret Service Best Practices for Seizing Electronic Evidence.

Documenting the Seizure.

Whether you are law enforcement or civilian, if the acquisition of computer equipment involves or may involve controversy, you should document taking possession of the equipment. This includes:

- Date seized
- Time seized
- Placed seized
- Who seized
- Who was present
- Who had access
- Who handled
- Where it was stored
- How it was stored
- Records of it being stored

Each one of these areas and activities should be recorded in the final report.

PROTECTION OF THE EVIDENCE

Once the equipment has been acquired or seized, it is your responsibility to maintain the integrity of that equipment. Your responsibility includes:

1. Preventing damage to the device
2. Preventing contamination of the data
3. Documenting protection of the evidence

You should have all preparations made in advance and not wait until the equipment has been acquired to figure out what to do with it.

Once the System and Storage Devices Have Been Secured,

You may then take the necessary steps to capture the information. To do this you should;

- Use forensically sound, proven recovery hardware and software
- Validate the integrity of the information capture using a recognized hashing algorithm
- Document your steps and results

There are numerous sound and credible forensic analysis tools available. Although there are several credible and highly effective forensic analysis packages, two of the most popular include Encase, by Guidance Software, and Forensic Toolkit, by Access Data.

The learner of this program should become familiar with other commercial products such as OnTrack, Encase and hardware acquisition systems. The forensic analysis program ILook is reserved for law enforcement only.

What the Forensic Examiner Tries to Recover

Although each disk drive or media device has its own use history, and due to the way the operating system processes, stores and retrieves data, there are various aspect of each drive that are prime targets for analysis. This includes

- Left over data files on the disk.
- Slack Space
- Swap Files
- Deleted Files
- Lost Files
- Corrupted Files

All of these are generally not recoverable and presented to the user by the operating system, however, as a recovered bit stream image under analysis, each is easily identified. Each of these aspects is also candidate for an operating system overwrite, thus, freezing the state of the system by pulling the plug is necessary to prevent loss of data.

Computer Forensic Analysis Systems

There are numerous types of computer forensic systems available and many forensic examiners custom build their own. To be a forensic analysis and recovery system, they all have some things in common.

A forensic analysis system can not permit the writing of data back to the drive or device under analysis. Thus, a write blocker must be inserted between the media and the system board interface. There are numerous types of write blockers and include USB, Floppy, IDE, SATA, SCSI and others.

Some forensic analysis and acquisition systems are referred to as a FRED system. FRED is an acronym for Forensic Recovery of Evidence Drive.

FRED System

Figure 14

Other Data Acquisition Devices

FRED systems are not the only media acquisition devices. There are numerous portable hardware devices that will perform a fast acquisition without requiring the drive to be removed from the system or relocated back to the forensics laboratory. An advantage of using this type of acquisition device is the speed at which it can acquire information.

One such device is the Hardcopy II by Voom Technologies. This device has the following capabilities:

- It can create a drive image of an ATA drive at speeds up to 5.5 GB per minute

- It will store an entire image in single ISO type file
  (ISO files can be used for forensic analysis)

- It will permit the partitioning of data into multiple files
  (This will accommodate archiving needs of very large image files)

- A CRC and an MD5 is created for each partition
  (This provides validation of the acquired data)

- Automatically image Host Protected Areas

- Laptop drives or SATA drives can be imaged

The benefits of these capabilities is greatly appreciated by the forensic examiner when dealing with very large images, when dealing with multiple images, or when performing on-site acquisitions.

Concepts of Acquisition, Analysis and Storage of a Target Media

1. The first step in a forensic analysis is to secure the environment. This includes the local area, the system and the disk drive. This is to prevent any inadvertent or intentional use of the system. Using a system that is desired to be forensically examined will alter the storage environment. Practically every user action on a system can potentially write data to the drive, thus possibly overwriting files.

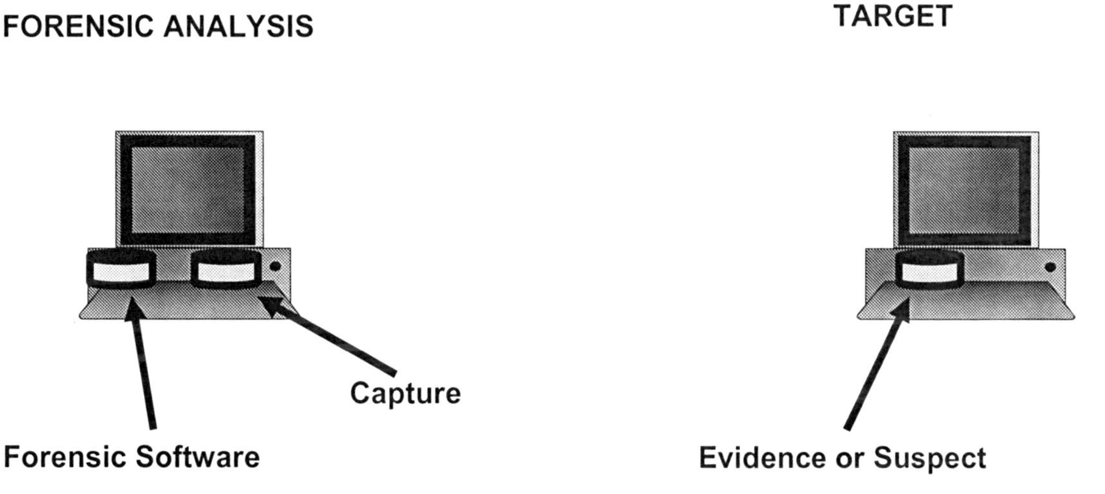

Figure 15

2. Once the environment has been secured, the evidence or target drive should be removed and placed in a forensic recovery system for duplication of the drive image.

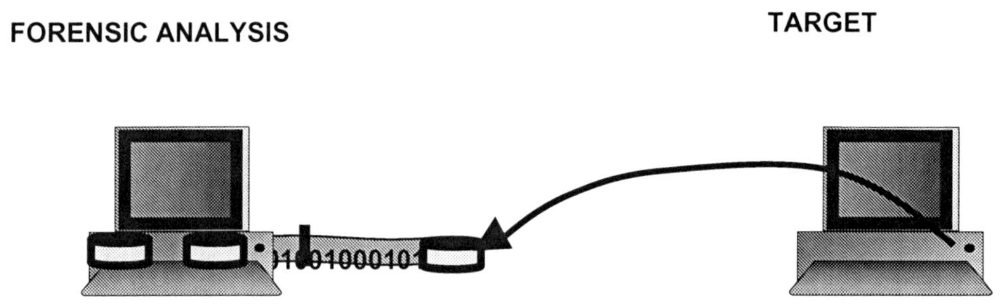

Figure 16

3. Once the drive has been inserted into the system an image can be acquired.

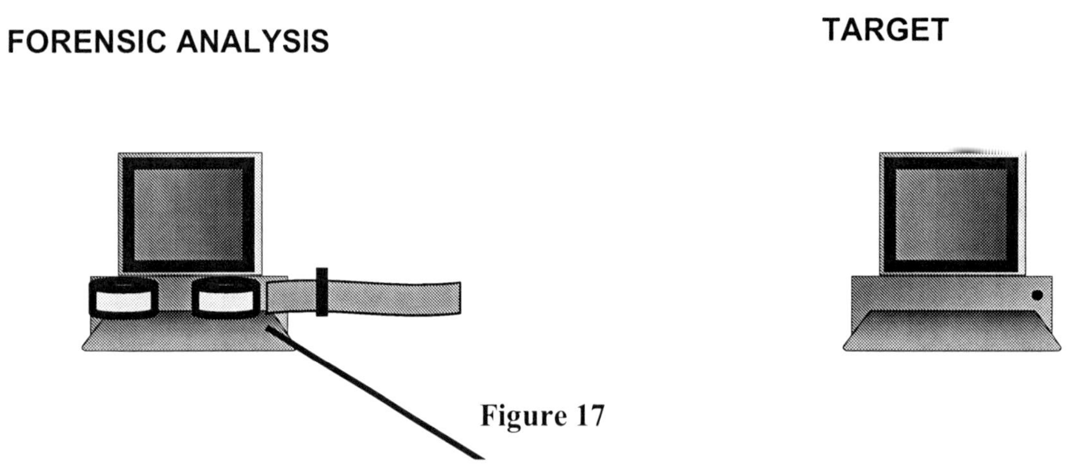

Figure 17

4. After the acquisition has been achieved, the drive should be stored in a secure location and the chain-of-custody documentation updated to reflect proper handling and storage.

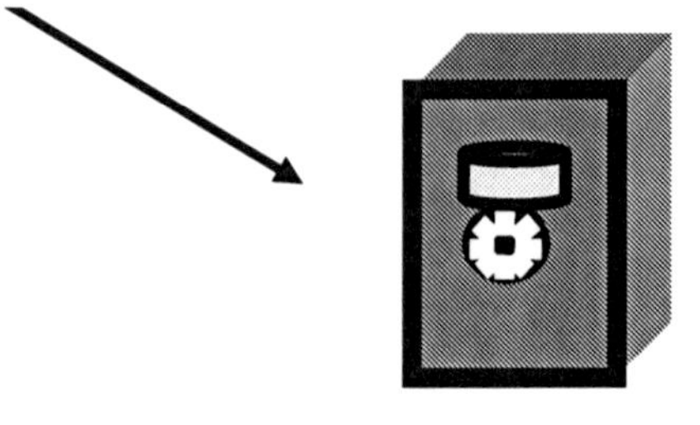

Figure 18

Forensic Analysis System

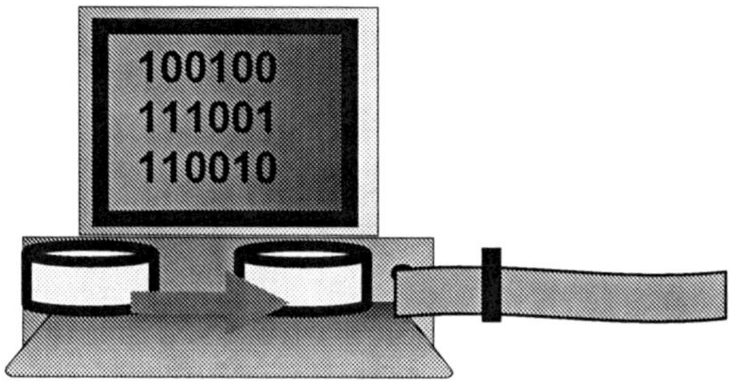

Figure 19

5. The drive image can then be analyzed.

6. After the analysis the report is generated and provided to the responsible party (client, employer).

Figure 20

Non-Forensic Recovery Tools

There are numerous file and photo recovery tools available for download from the Internet. Caution must be exercised when using tools of unknown origin or may not have been proven in previous forensic examination. Some recovery tools will permit recovery of information but at the expense of writing to the drive. This is not forensically sound.

Locate and download the RecoveryMyFiles from the Internet. Install this program on your hard drive. Once installed and initialized, Select Fast File Search

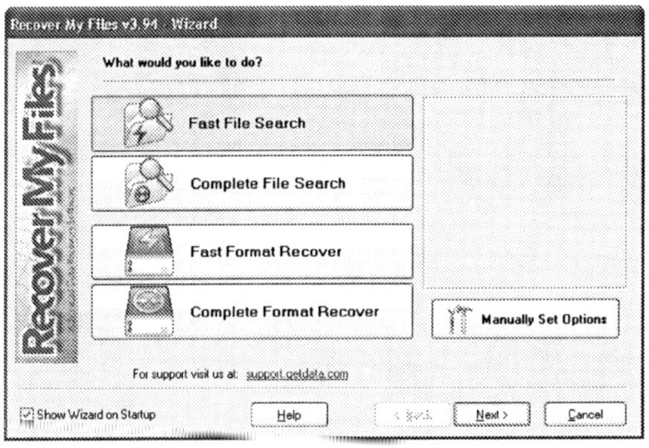

Figure 21

Then select a particular type of graphic file to search.

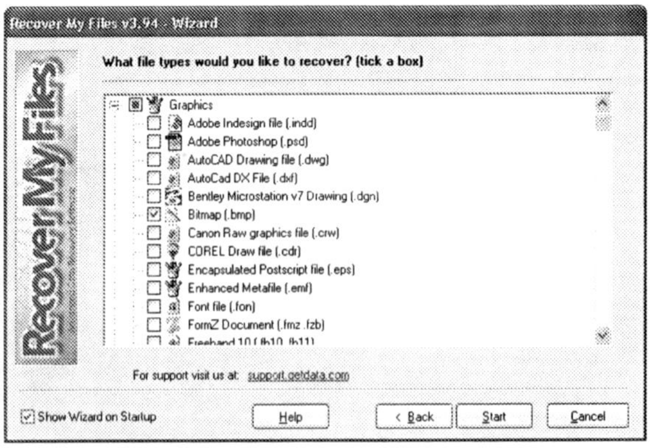

Figure 22

Next, select a particular type of document file to search.

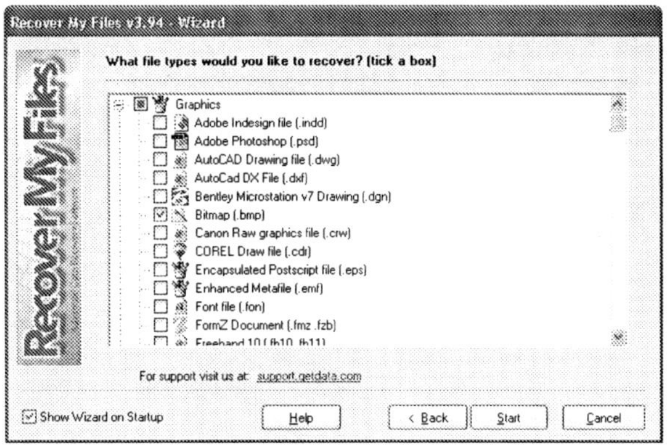

Figure 23

The program will begin searching for files on the hard disk that may have been deleted.

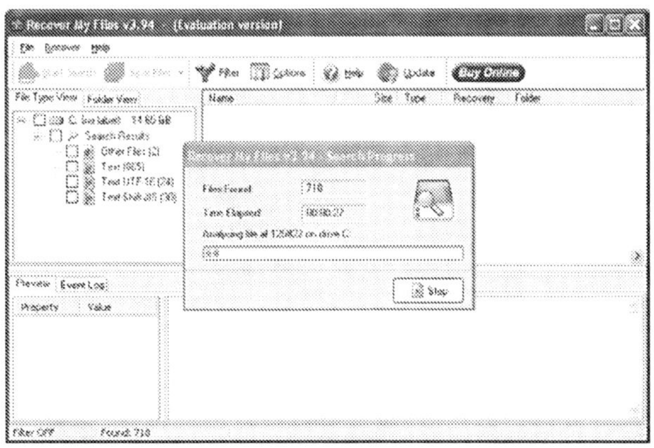

Figure 24

One of the aspects of data and file recovery from a system is to keep confidential the information that you may recover. Much personal information may be discovered and it is with the mandate of professional ethics that a forensic examiner not share the specifics of their findings with others. In some cases this is not possible or even appropriate. Discovery of illegal or improper materials may need to be brought to the attention of the proper authorities, (management, system owner, law enforcement). Use discretion in this area.

What Did We Accomplish by These Steps?

These Steps Just Accomplished

1. We modified the operating system by installing a program to it
2. By installing this program, we overwrote files on disk
3. By installing this program, we modified the FAT / MFT and the Registry

"THIS IS NOT FORENSICALLY SOUND!"

And should never be done on an evidence or source drive.

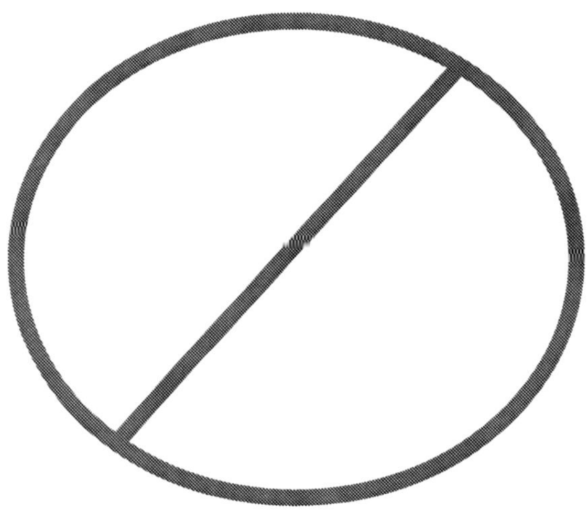

Importance of the Windows Registry

No explanation of a personal computer would be adequate without an introduction to the Windows Registry. The Windows Registry is a database that contains hardware, operating system and application setting information. It also contains information most computer users do not know about, that of system user information.

The Windows Registry is a very complex but logical structure that is comprised of components called keys. There are five main keys that contain what seems like an unlimited amount of subkeys. Some of these subkeys contain subkeys of their own.

What makes the Registry a gold mine of information is that it tells the actual story of system use and configuration. Even if the incriminating files are erased and unrecoverable, the Registry may reveal that the file was downloaded, installed, where it was downloaded from, what software was installed or uninstalled, and a range of other information. If a user claims, "I did not type in that web address", there is a Registry key that identifies typed URL's, or Uniform Resource Locators, also known as web addresses.

If a user claims they did not insert their USB, also known as a flash or thumb drive, into a particular computer, the Registry can identify which flash drives, including model, make and serial number of any thumb drive connected to and registered by the operating system. Additionally, connected network drives, Start – Run programs, Open Files, System Security, Application and Event Logs are recoverable by this simple batch file. The Registry may be the pot of gold at the end of a digital rainbow.

The Registry maintains records of almost everything that happens on the computer. This includes what programs have been installed, what programs have been uninstalled, what hardware has been connected to the computer, including hard disk drives, CD-ROM drives, DVD drives, USB (thumb) drives, and other devices.

Additionally, Internet searches, typed web addresses, what documents have been opened and how often they have been opened is recorded in the Registry. So, to put this into perspective, a person who desires to keep this information confidential would target key aspects of the Registry.

The One's and Zeros of Disk Technology

To understand what a forensic analysis is, one must understand how data is written and recovered to and from a disk drive. This includes understanding how data is written, stored, overwritten and retrieved from magnetic storage media.

As data is written to the disk drive it is done so as a stream of magnetic fields with the polarity of each field determining if the individual magnetic representation is interpreted as a binary 0 or 1. The bit patterns are written on the disk as either formatting (addressing) information or as data. The formatting information includes identification of data containers, known as sectors and clusters. The data is placed inside of the boundaries of these containers (sectors and clusters) and the location of that data is recorded in a locator table known as a File Allocation Table (FAT) or Master File Table (MFT). These tables may be compared to a telephone book where the title of the contents is recorded with the address.

It is important to understand that the FAT and MFT do not store the data, only the address of the data. If the FAT or MFT is corrupted or overwritten, the data may still be located elsewhere on the disk. The operating system relies on the FAT and MFT to locate this data.

Media, Disk Structures and Drive Geometry

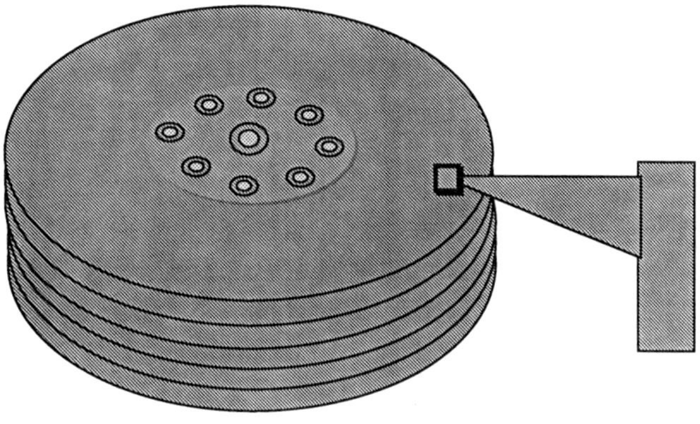

Figure 25

The logical structure of a disk drive involves the mapping of the surface of the media for the storage, identification and recovery of data and information. The surface of a disk drive consists of the following:

Tracks: Circular patterns of data and information on the disk. Track 1 is different from track 2. Track 3 is different from track 4. Each of these tracks may contain user or system files.

Cylinder: Circular patterns of data and information on the disk that consist of the same track number but across multiple platters. Track 1 on platter 1 and track 1 on platter 2 and track 1 on platter 3 comprise cylinder 1.

Sector: A sector is a pie shaped portion of data on the disk. A sector is typically 512 bytes in size.

Head: The head is the device that provides the read and write operations for the disk. A tiny core of wire wrapped into a spiral or cylindrical shape creates the magnetic field as current passes through it. Current passing from one direction may leave a North-South imprint on the media while current passing in the opposite direction may leave a

South-North imprint. These N-S and S-N imprints are interpreted as a 1 or 0 when recovered.

Platter: The platter is the physical portion of the disk that consists of a rigid and extremely smooth surface of a magnetic coating such as oxide. This oxide coating retains the magnetic imprint left by the read / write head.

Cluster: A cluster consists of sectors and is the addressable unit on the media by the operating system. Some operating systems will write data in clusters consisting of 2 sectors. Some will write clusters sizes up to 65,000 bytes.

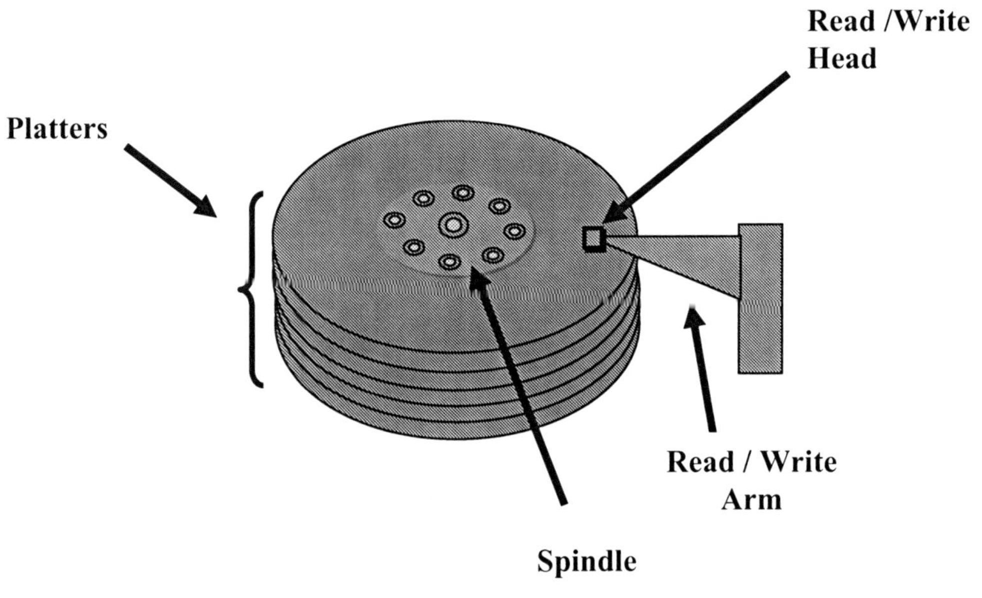

Figure 26

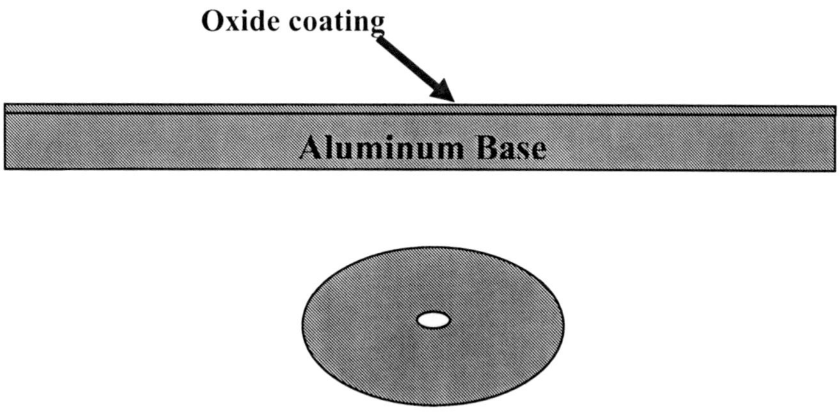

Figure 27

The construction of a disk platter is based upon a rigid surface coated with some form of oxide that will retain the magnetic imprints impressed by the influence of the magnetic fields produced by the read / write head.

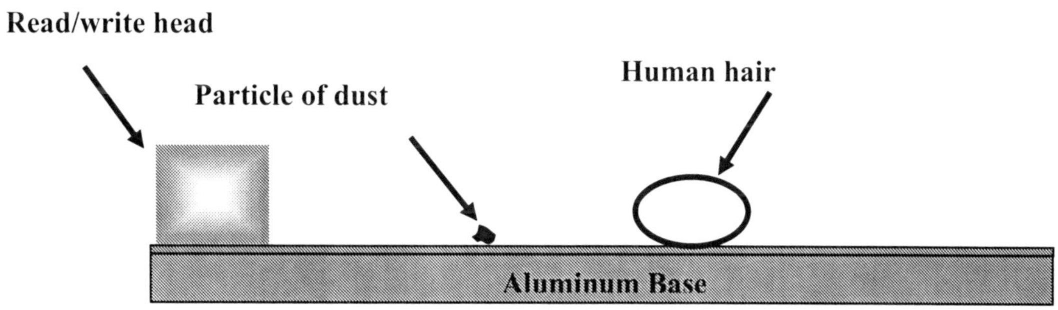

Figure 28

The read / write head fly's above the surface of the disk platter. As the disk spins a cushion of air pushes the head above the surface and it rides on this air cushion.

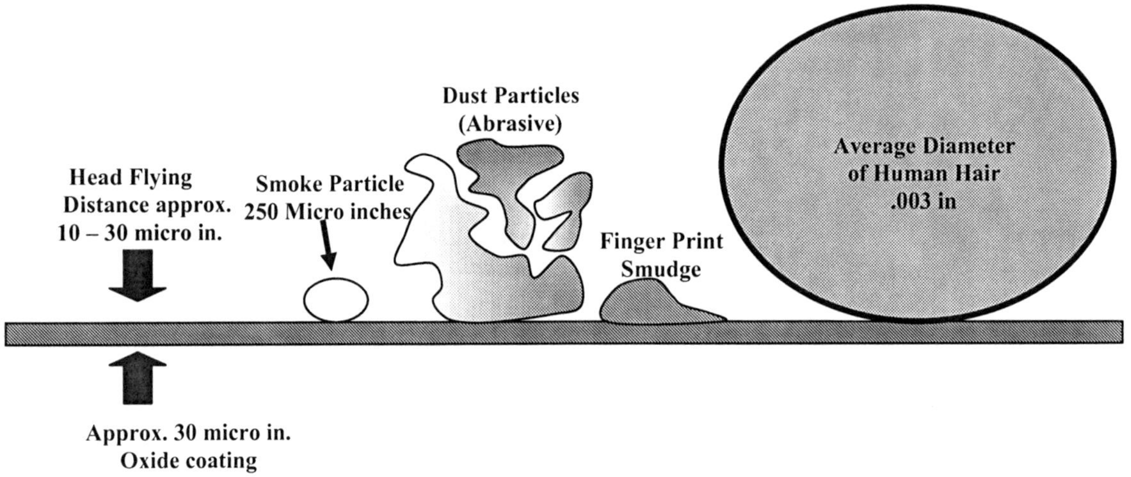

Figure 29

The tolerances are incredibly close and precise to where there is no room for any outside contaminant to pass between them. If some particle does, the head and or the particle impacts the disk. This is known as a head or disk crash.

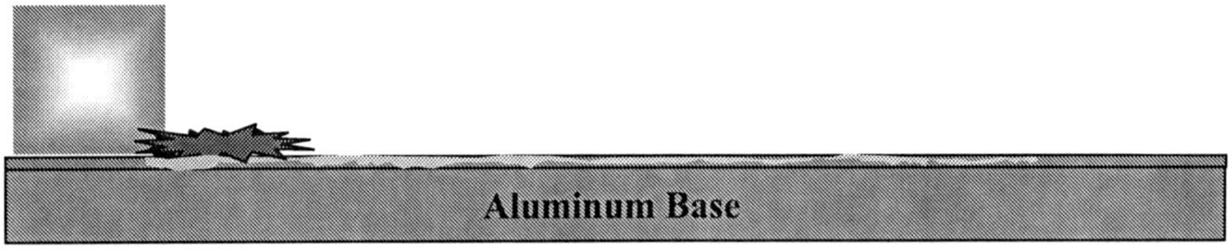

Figure 30

If this happens, microscopic particles of oxide may be scraped off, thus creating additional contaminants within the drive that may also impact the head.

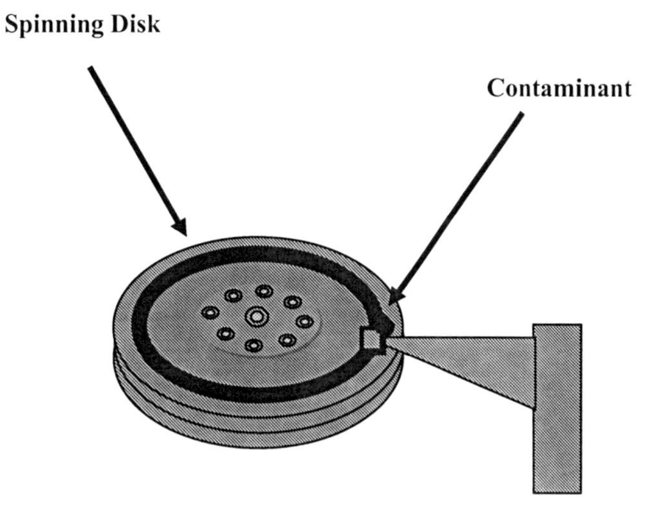

Figure 31

As the disk continues to spin, the contaminants continue to spin as well. Eventually, the surface of the disk will be damaged to the point that a wear or damage circular pattern will be made.

Tape Technology

Magnetic recording on tape works the same way, except tape media is flexible and can be rolled into spools. These spools had the effect of providing a significantly larger surface area of media while still small physically. Most tape technology has been replaced by higher capacity disk drives and solid state storage such as USB thumb drives.

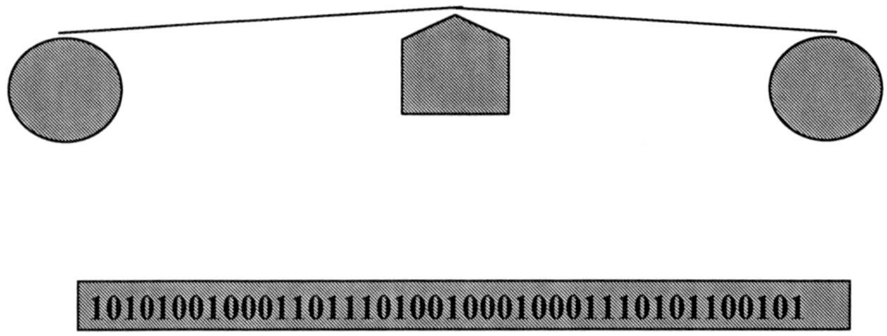

Tape
(Top View)

Figure 32

Magnetic tape works on the same principle except with tape technology the media actually rides on the surface of the head and the media is flexible instead of a rigid surface like a disk drive.

Tape
(Side View)

Figure 33

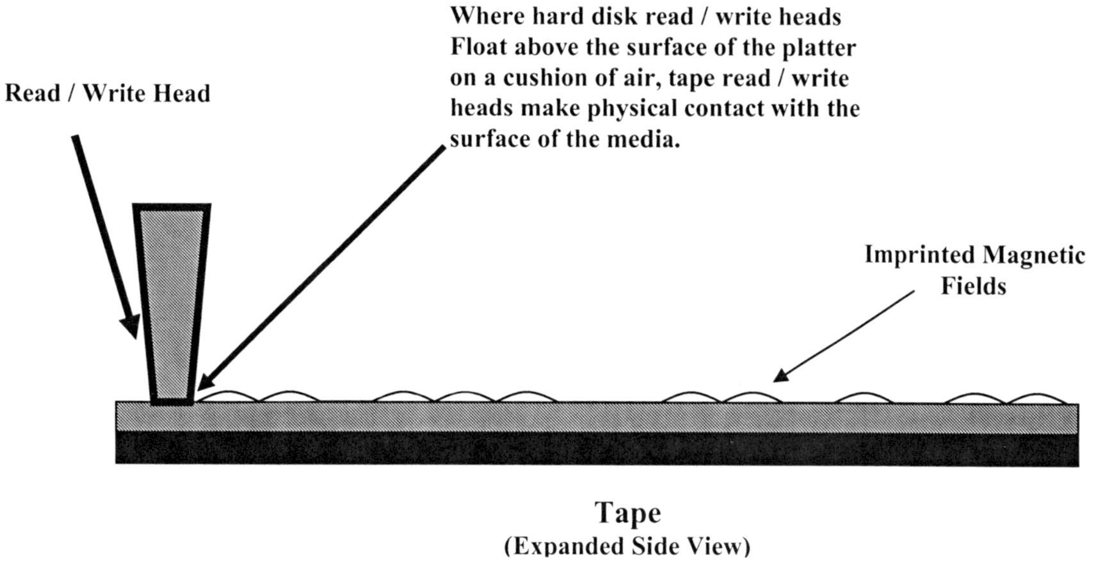

Figure 34

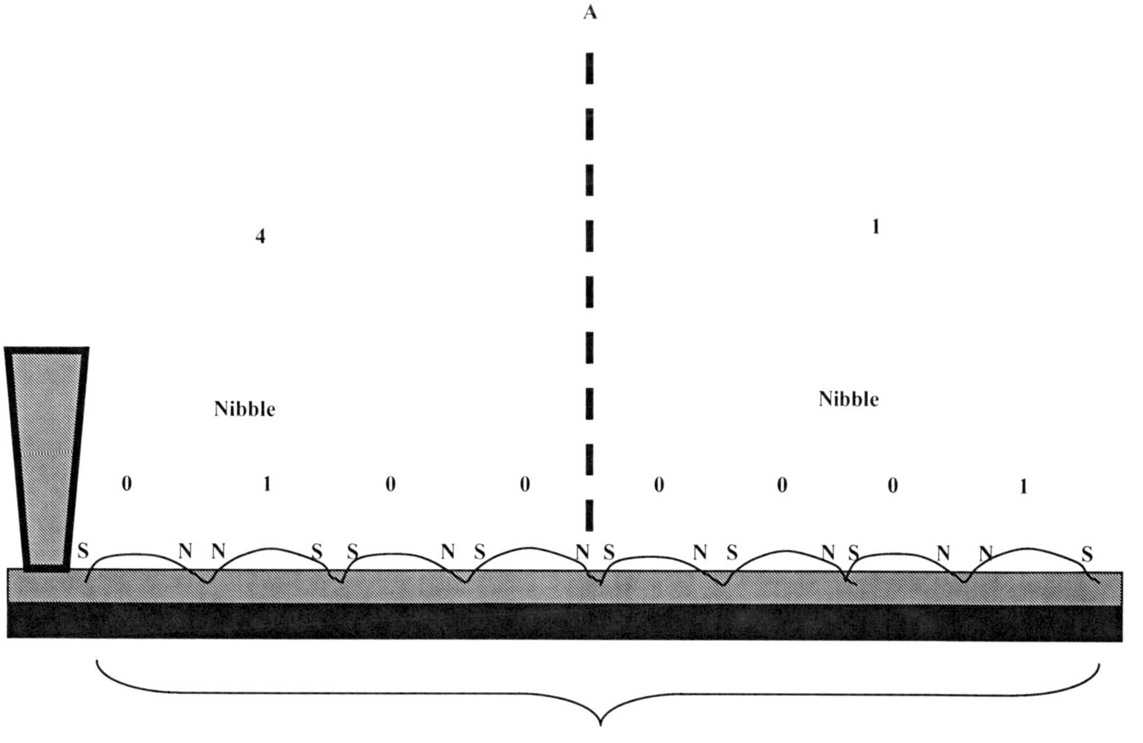

Figure 35

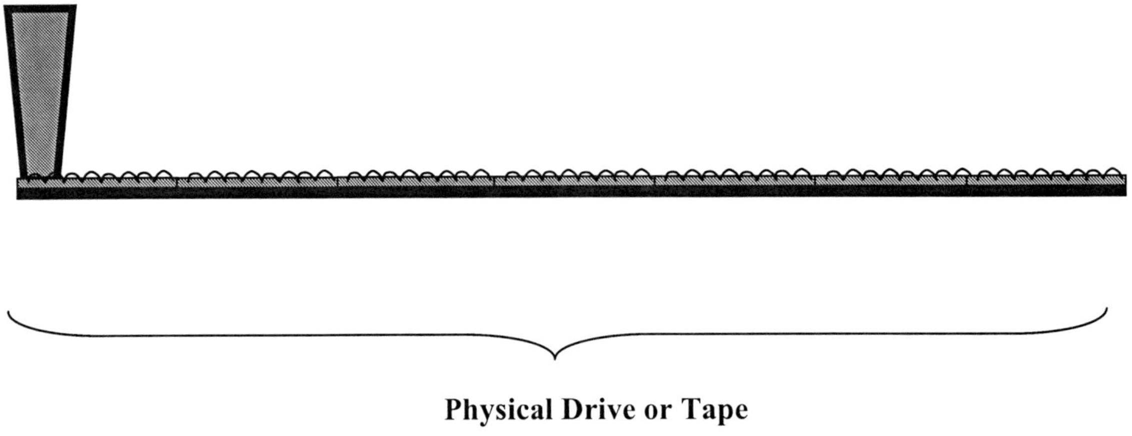

Figure 36

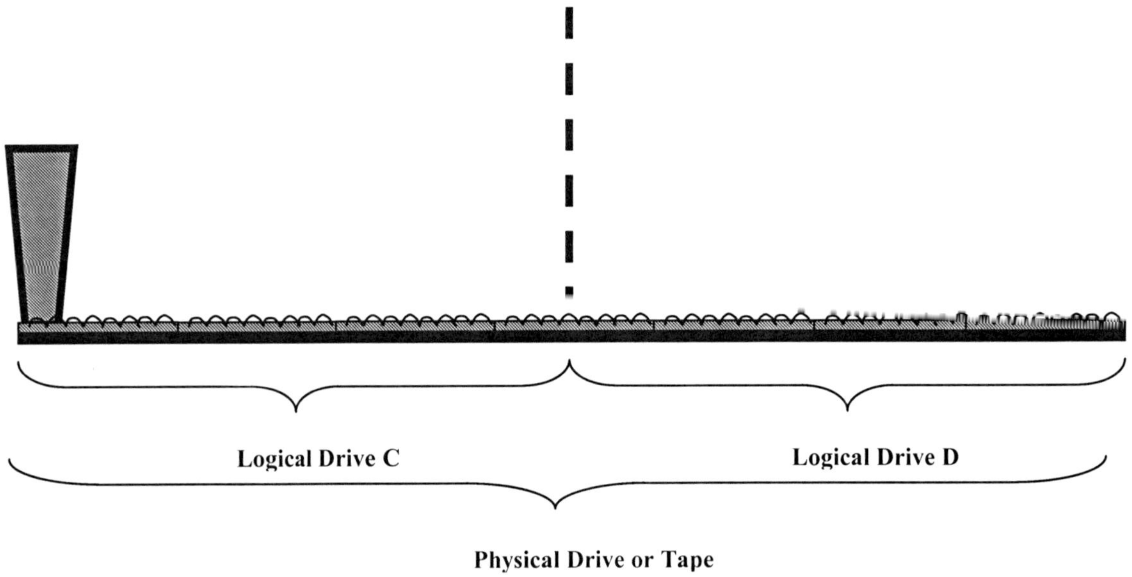

Figure 37

Handling and Construction

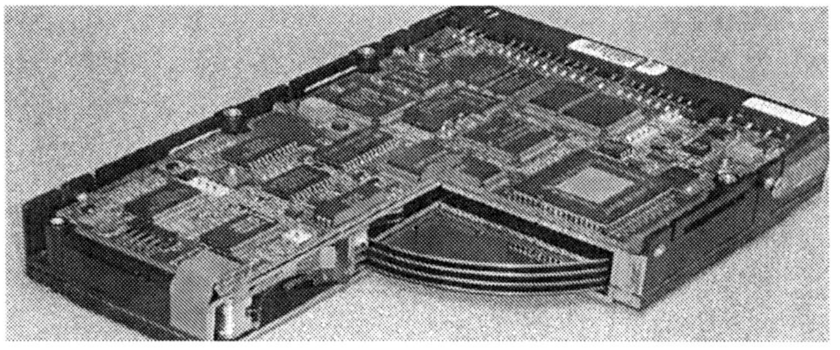

Figure 38

Cut away view of a hard disk drive exposing the platters (media) and the physical construction of the device.

Figure 39

The same drive but with a side view.

Securing an electronic device requires a bit more understanding as to the technology when it comes to how to secure it. Seizure of computer not only includes protecting the physical equipment but the information as well. A magnet does not effect a ceramic coffee cup or a piece of paper, but it will erase and may even destroy a hard disk. A high enough voltage can alter the contents of a hard disk and as versatile as electronic data is, it is highly susceptible to magnetic fields. Moving electronics, electricity, create magnetic fields.

Computer equipment must be protected from exposure to weather elements as well. Moisture can short out the electronic connections and physically damage the equipment. This includes voltages generated by the human body. Humans are electric generators in the right conditions and demonstrate this every time they get a shock when touching a door handle or when shaking hands with someone else. This is why ESD, or Electro-Static Discharge precautions must be maintained when handling. Storing disk drives in non-conductive bags, also known as anti-static bags, works best. These bags are metal impregnated and conduct electricity, which prevents it from building up a charge.

Perhaps one of the best law enforcement guidelines on seizing electronic evidence can be found in the publication provided by the United States Secret Service. This document, titled Best Practices for Seizing Electronic Evidence, and can be found at the web site http://www.secretservice.gov/electronic_evidence.shtml. Essentially, this document provides Secret Service guidelines on how to secure an electronic crime scene and parallel the following steps:

1. **Secure the scene**. This may include isolation from the Internet. If a computer or network technical person is available you may decide to solicit their assistance in the matter of isolating the computer from the rest of the cyberspace.

2. **Secure the computer as if it is evidence**. This includes photographing the computer, front and back, including the connecting cables and what is on the screen. Physical connections between the evidence system and the network connection should be photographed. Additional media in the vicinity of the system may reveal information pertinent to the case at hand. All of this is potential information and potential evidence.

To freeze the state of the computer it is necessary to unplug the computer from the power source. It should be unplugged at the system, not at the wall. Many systems are connected to UPS, or Uninterruptable Power Supplies which will trigger an automatic operating system shutdown sequence with the operating system if a loss of power is detected. However, before unplugging the system and depending upon time restrictions, you may need to investigate if the system has an internal UPS source. If this is the situation, you would need to unplug the disk drive first or unplug the internal power supply, depending upon specific circumstances.

The importance of pulling the plug versus shutting the system down is that during a normal Windows operating system shutdown, files are written to the disk that maintain the state of the operating system. This is in order for the system to remember where it was at when it is loaded again. Pulling the power plug makes the shut down sequence impossible and creates a time line of events. What was on the drive when you pulled the plug is still on the drive. If adequate precautions are taken, it is impossible to add any additional information to the drive after this point. Thus, you have frozen the state of the system in time.

3. **Secure the equipment for transport.** Take the entire system, not just the hard drive. Proper forensics evaluation back at the lab can then reveal the contents of the drive. Your traditional chain-of-custody procedures would be applicable as well.

Once the seized equipment is in the forensics laboratory, additional precautions and steps are employed to maintain the integrity of the data and to acquire it without alteration.

Isolation and Preservation

Disconnecting a system of interest from the Internet may be key to preserving the integrity of the data on the disk drive. This is a time sensitive situation and subject to human decision. The contents of volatile memory, RAM, may be updated or modified even while the attending officer is standing next to it. Although any updates would be minor, it is still dynamic. Additionally, it is entirely possible that another human, not within the proximity of the room the computer is located, may be connected to that system and changing files. Granted, most cases do not involve immediate sensitivity of this level, however, it must be appreciated that some involving issues of financial crimes, national security or cyber terrorism.

Dealing with Unknown Media and Files

The field of computer engineering has taught me to be empirical. This applies to the handling of electronic devices and includes removable media such as floppy disks, CD-ROM disks and USB (thumb) drives.

Technology has become more interactive with humankind because it has become more automated and user friendly. Even the non-techies have access to tools and techniques only government spies and computer engineers understood just a few decades ago. The number of possible configurations, concealing tools and techniques and booby trap scenarios is staggering.

When a CD or DVD is found at a potential crime scene it should be treated like it is booby trapped. That is, if installed into a system, the auto run feature of the operating system should be disabled. If the auto run feature is enabled on the operating system, an alternative method is available. Simply depressing the shift key while the CD or DVD is being loaded will negate any auto run activities. I have taught may future forensic examiners this lesson by setting up a system and leaving CD's with auto run features that shut down the examiners system once the CD has been inserted. Some bad guys take this much further by having the CD execute a program that will erase the examiners hard disk drive. Thus, requiring them to reinstall many thousands of dollars of licensed software.

Perform Forensics Lab # 3

TITLE: Protection of Evidence

OBJECTIVE:

To understand handling and storage procedures for protection of data, information and devices.

The Logical Disk Structure

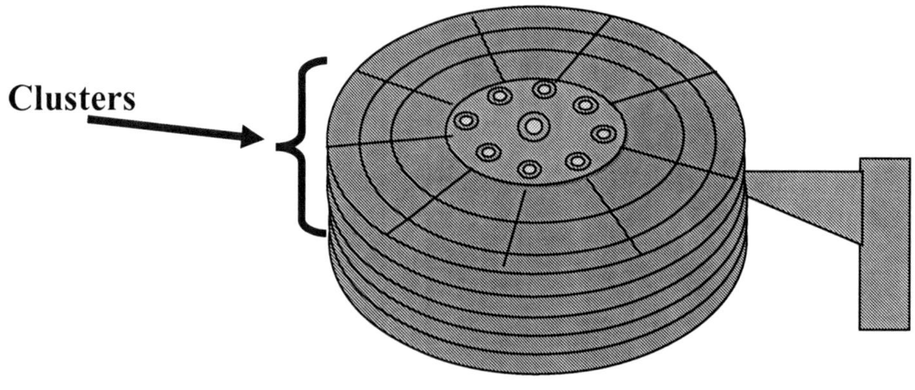

Figure 40

The logical format consists of sectors. Each sector or group of sectors is assigned to an addressable cluster. If a file is to be written to the disk that fills only one sector and the operating system writes clusters consisting of two sectors, then the remaining sector will consist of RAM slack.

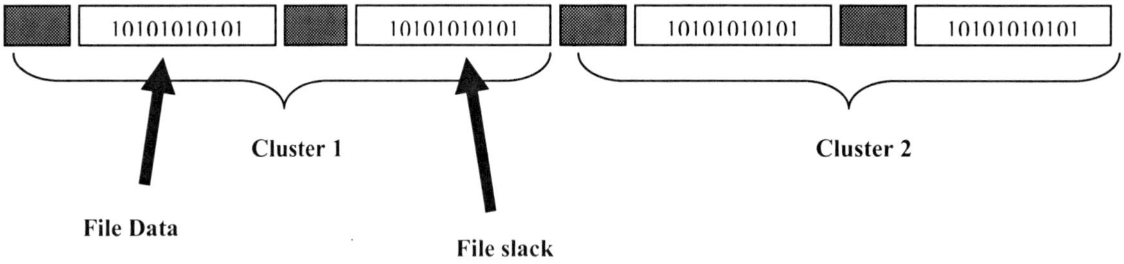

Figure 41

Left over data on this disk is known as file slack. File slack contains information left over from previous write operations.

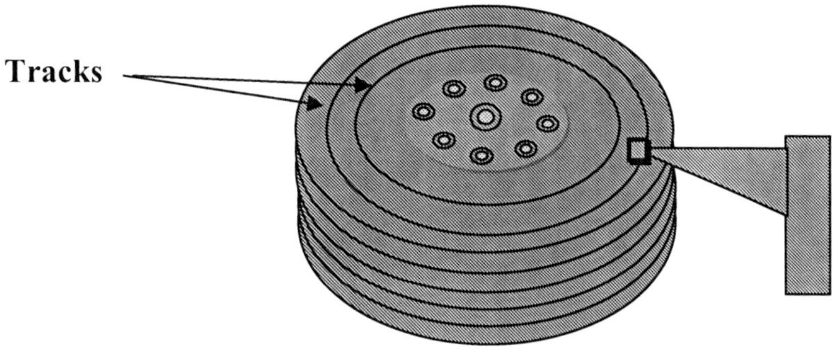

Figure 45

A track is a concentric circle of data and information on a disk. It is called a track because it is consistent and is circular due to the round and spinning nature of the disk drive. Track 1 is different from track 2. Track 3 is different from track 4. Each of these tracks may contain user or system files or only format patterns that the read / write head will follow for the future placement and recovery of information.

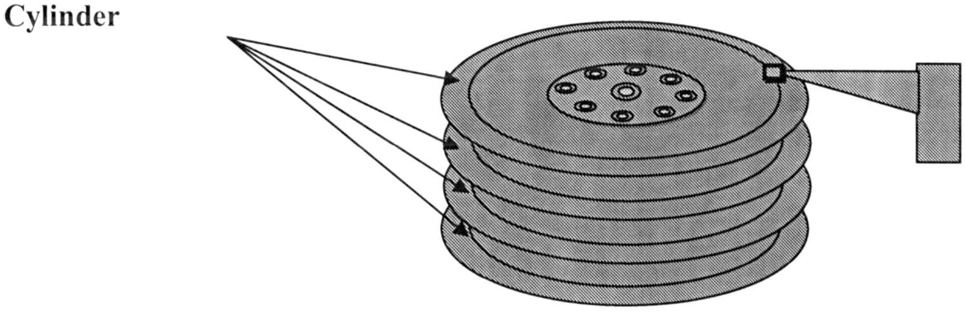

Figure 46

Cylinders are circular patterns of data and information on the disk that consist of the same track number but across multiple platters. Track 1 on platter 1 and track 1 on platter 2 and track 1 on platter 3 comprise cylinder 1.

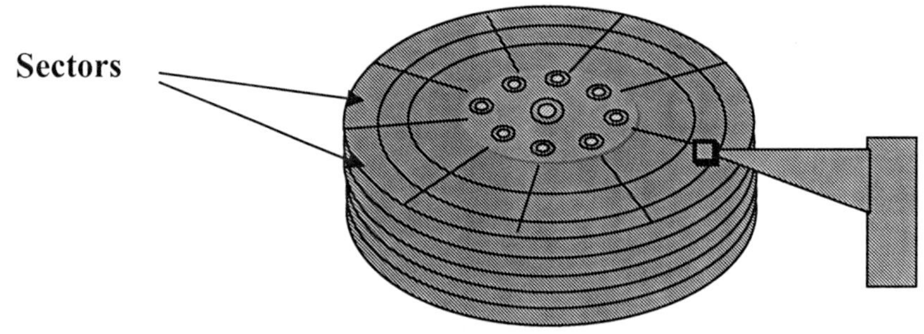

Figure 47

A sector is a pie shaped portion of data on the disk. A sector is typically 512 bytes in size.

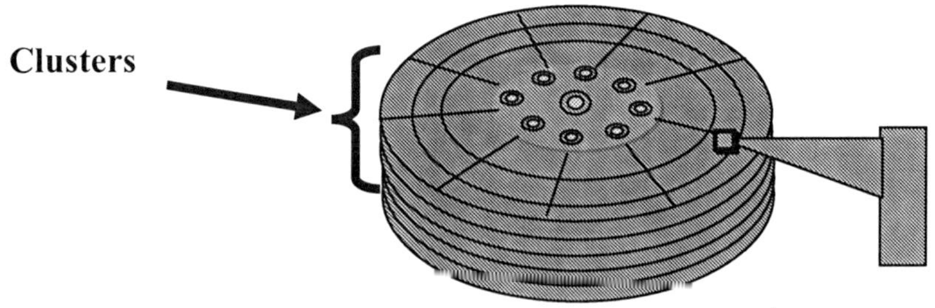

Figure 48

A cluster consists of sectors and is the addressable unit on the media by the operating system. Some operating systems will write data in clusters consisting of 2 sectors. Some will write clusters sizes up to 65,000 bytes.

Shadow Data

Another source of residual or left over data on the disk is that of shadow data. This type of data is not recoverable by traditional forensics software as forensics recovery software can only recover what the drive can read. However, in some cases that may involve national security issues, advanced technology and methods may be employed to recover shadow data.

Shadow data is the result of overwriting data and not being exact in the track spacing overwrite. This is due to the mechanical tolerances of the disk drive and the width of the read head. Remember, disk drives are not designed to erase data, they are designed to write data. The method of erasing is based upon overwriting.

On hard disks, data is written in tracks, the concentric circles of data. To better understand these tracks, picture an automobile driving through a fresh snow, with the tire tracks representing the data tracks. Now picture another car driving exactly over the previous cars tracks in an attempt to overwrite the tracks of the previous car. The first car represents the original data written on the disk. The second car represents an attempt to overwrite the tracks of the first car with new data. The results will be, no matter how precise the driver of the second car, the second tracks will not 100% cover the first tracks. In essence, a very small sliver of data from the first track will still be resident on the disk. Any data pattern found between the new track and the original track represents shadow data.

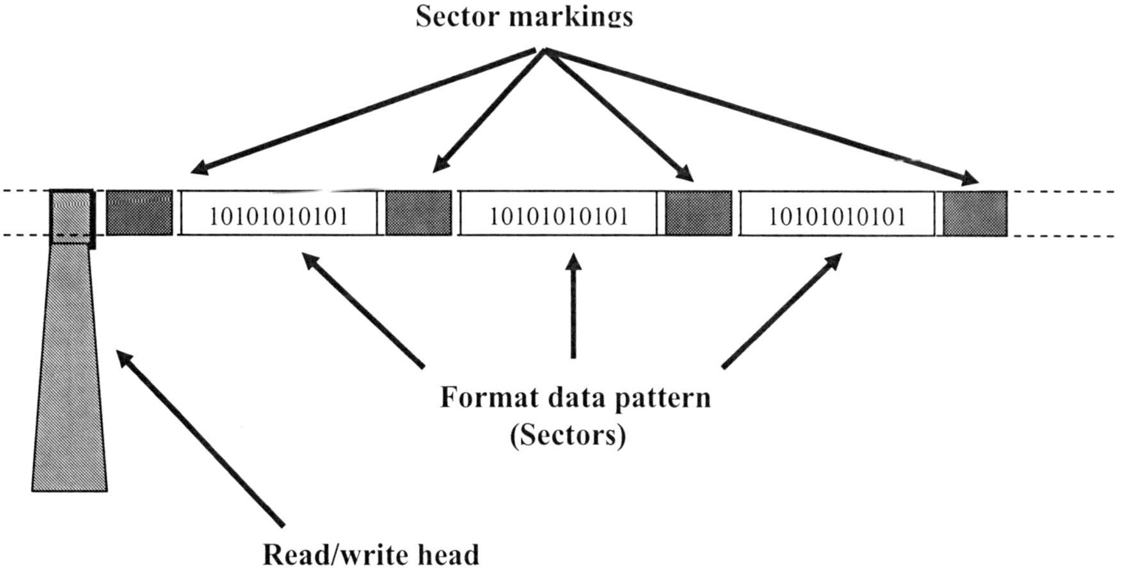

Figure 42

Figure 42 demonstrate the relationship between the data pattern as written on the disk or tape and the read / write head of the disk drive. The broken line represents the original width of the data track as written on the disk.

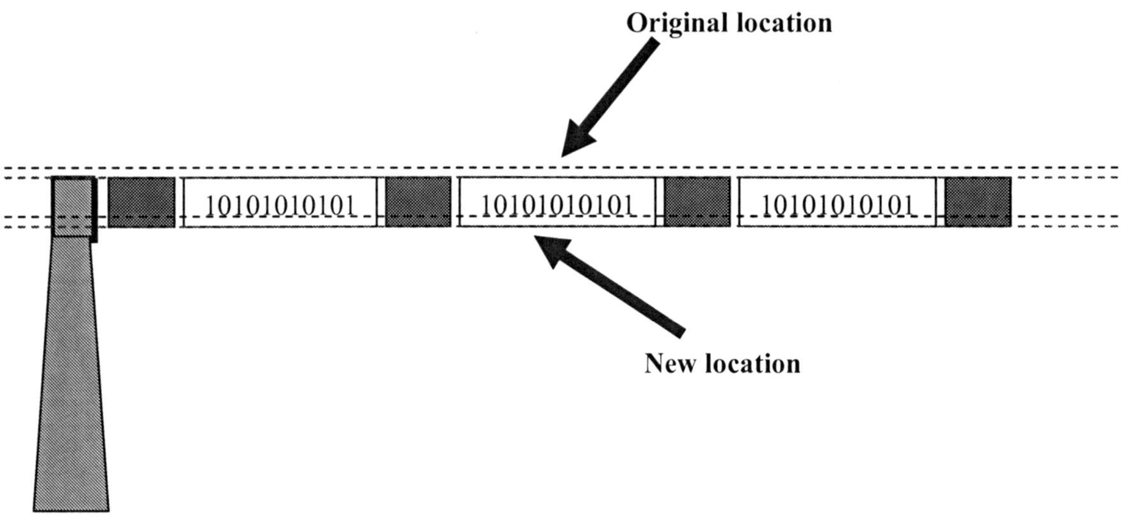

Figure 43

Figure 43 demonstrates an overwrite operation by the read / write head. Due to mechanical tolerances, this operation will not be 100% exact over the previously written track. Thus, a remnant of the original track may be present and adjacent to the overlay track.

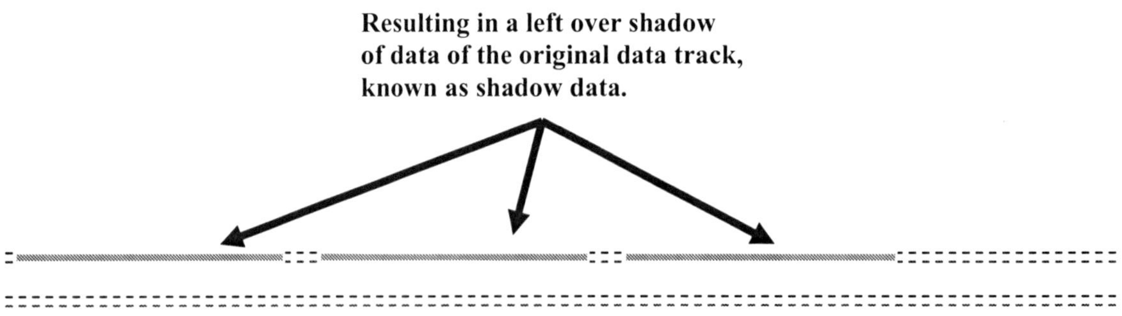

Figure 44

The result is a sliver of the previous tracks data pattern. If this previous sliver of information can be read, the overwritten information can be recovered. This data is not recoverable by commercial forensics analysis software and generally outside the realm of the computer forensics examiner. However, it is recoverable by scientific methods by using frequency analysis equipment found in government agencies and engineering firms who design disk drives. Generally this information might be of concern in cases of national security, but not divorce or lower level criminal cases.

Where Forensic Information Comes From

As previously stated, forensic analysis of a hard disk can reveal information not surrendered by the operating system. This information includes:

- Active files on the media
- Deleted files on the media
- Partially overwritten files on the media
- File autosave operations
- Swap files
- File slack
- Lost clusters
- RAM data that is used to fill the buffer during a write operation

Analyzing and recovery of this type of information provides an electronic snapshot of the disk use and history.

Disk Fragmentation

Files can be "shuffled" by the user and the operating system and as they get written, deleted, overwritten, relocated and sometimes, but rarely, lost on various types of media, the disk becomes fragmented. Thus, due to multiple read, write and delete operations, files eventually may not be placed on the media in a continuous or consecutive pattern. When this happens, the file is fragmented.

Individually fragmented files are not a concern. However, thousands or tens of thousands of fragmented files is a concern. When this happens, the media is considered 'Fragmented', and overall performance suffers.

Example of a Continuous File

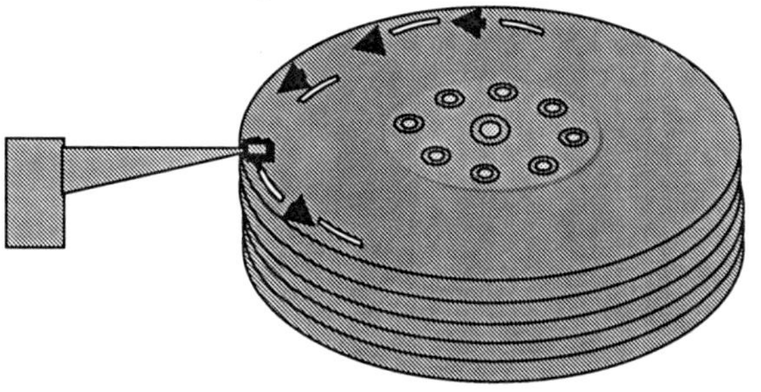

Figure 49

A continuous file is one that is directly connected, or physically chained together sector to sector and cluster to cluster. All parts of a file are logically chained, but they may be fragmented by being dispersed in various parts of the disk drive.

Example of a Fragmented File

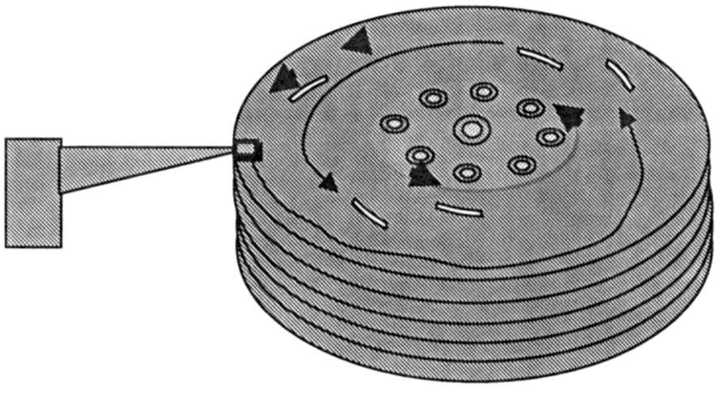

Figure 50

A fragmented file is one that is not physically contiguous and various clusters may be dispersed throughout the surface of the media. Although this is no challenge for the operating system, when many thousands of files are fragmented, the response time for a read or write operation is degraded.

Example of a Cross-Linked Cluster
Two Unrelated Clusters Point to the Same Cluster

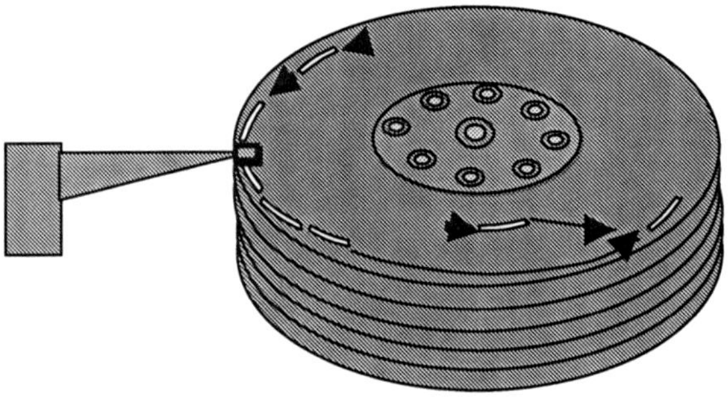

Figure 51

Cross-linked clusters is a phenomenon more likely to be seen in older operating systems. When the operating system gets confused and parts of two files point to the same cluster, the file is fragmented.

System Utility Programs for Disk Drives

Scandisk

Scandisk is a utility program that may re-link cross-linked clusters. This application will also perform a read of the disk surface and report any difficult to read or noon-recoverable portions on the disk. This should never be performed on an evidence drive.

Defragment

A software utility program that can re-sequence files to make them consecutive. Like a Scandisk operation, this should never be performed on an evidence drive.

How Data is Stored on a Disk Drive

The difference between information and data is that data is raw facts. Information consists of data. At it's lowest level, data is written as bits. Eight bits equals one byte and 512 bytes equals one sector.

Information is recorded in the FAT as clusters with each cluster equivalent to at least two sectors. A file that is only 512 bytes long will leave one entire sector of slack in a cluster. This slack may consist of left over data from RAM information and may not pertain to the particular file.

Finding the Data on the Media

11010010 10001011 11100010 11010101 11110001 11110011
11010101 11110001 11110011 11010010 10001011 11100010
11110001 11110011 11010010 10001011 10001011 11100010

One Byte

Figure 52

As explained previously, data is recorded on a disk drive in a hierarchal manner. At the lowest level data is recorded as individual bits. Eight bits is equivalent to one byte.

11110001

Eight Bits

Figure 53

11110001

Two Nibbles

Figure 54

One byte is equivalent to two nibbles. The reason nibbles are significant is that the highest value in the hexadecimal numbering system is F, which is equivalent to the number 15. It takes four ones, or, 1111 to make the number 15 in hexadecimal.

11010010 10001011 11100010 11010101 11110001 1111001 11010010 10001011 11100010

512 Bytes = One Sector

Between 2 & 65,536 Sectors = One Cluster

Figure 55

Additionally, data on the Media is Addressed and Stored as Clusters in the FAT or MFT. The FAT or MFT is the equivalent of a telephone book for the disk drive. It records the location of every file by name and cluster address location on the media. If a file is on the disk but not listed in the FAT or MFT, it is considered as being in unallocated space.

FAT or MFT →

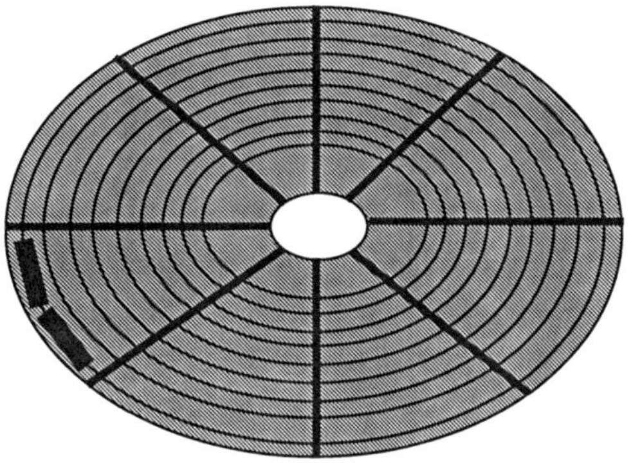

Figure 56

Familiarity with the Command Line

Forensic examinations frequently require the use of and some forensic software requires the use of the command line. Use of the command line is commonly referred to as the DOS command line. Technically, in Windows XP and above, this is not technically correct. DOS, an acronym for Disk Operating System, was the first major PC operating system in the U.S. market. The influence of DOS has reaching effects even today.

The acronym DOS is generally associated with the Windows 9X operating system series, such as Windows 95, 98 and ME. These operating systems used evolutions of the original DOS operating system as their platform. Windows XP and later operating system provide the option of using the DOS or FAT operating based system, or the NTFS (New Technology File System) operating based system. DOS uses FAT, an acronym for File Allocation Table while NTFS generally uses MFT, or the Master File Table. Both serve as reoad maps to files on the disk. It should be noted that NFTS provides the option of utilizing FAT during formatting and installation of the operating system where DOS or Windows 9X does not provide this capability.

To become proficient in data acquisition and recovery, it is critical that the examiner be familiar with each of the following commands:

RD	ATTRIB	DISKCOPY	DATE
TIME	DIR	PAUSE	RENAME
TYPE	DEL	FDISK	VER
DOSKEY	EDIT	PROMPT	PATH
FC	TYPE	LABEL	VOL
DEFRAG	ECHO	XCOPY	MEM
SYS	REM	MOVE	SCANDISK
EXIT	FORMAT	PRINT	HELP
ARP	DELTREE	NBTSTAT	ROUTE PRINT
NETSTAT /?			

Some of these commands display the contents of volatile memory (RAM) while others will alter the files and contents of the disk. Again, it is imperative that the forensic examiner understand that they must never use any command that will alter the surface of an evidence or source drive that may be under analysis. Forensics Lab # 4 will provide the opportunity to become better acquainted with these native operating system command.

Perform Forensics Lab # 4

TITLE: Using the Windows Command Line

OBJECTIVE:

Become familiar with each command listed. Create a batch file to demonstrate understanding of command line scripting.

Overview of Data Structures and File Formats

1101001010001110101001100100100101010101001
1111001000100111001001000101010101011001011
111100100010011010101001010010010010111101
1110010010101110001010101010100111110001010

There are countless types of data and file format structures and it is not possible to learn all of them with specific recall ability. However, this section will explain the concept so the examiner will understand how to learn future files and structures.

Understanding Data Structure and File Formats Using Debug

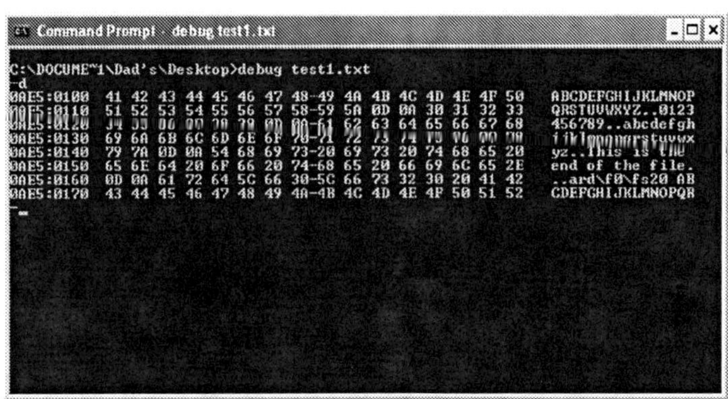

Figure 57

It is important to understand the relationship between binary, hexadecimal and human readable characters. Binary is the two state numbering system used by digital computers. Hexadecimal is the base 16 numbering system and is a convenient method of categorizing binary strings into some form of useful information. ASCII is an acronym for American Standard Code for Information Interchange. It is a scheme for having specific types of binary patterns or hexadecimal values represent certain types of human readable characters or commands.

Binary		Hexadecimal		ASCII
0100 0001	=	41	=	A
0100 0010	=	42	=	B
0100 0011	=	43	=	C
0100 0100	=	44	=	D

To better understand this relationship, perform an on-line search for ASCII chart. Here you will observe the many variances of characters and hexadecimal values that represent each character.

For many years ASCII was the standard for character recognition between systems and still is, however, as the global environment has grown, so has the need for characters other than what has been provided in the ASCII standard. Now, ASCII is a subset of a much bigger set of character representations known as Unicode.

Once you have acquired an ASCII chart, consider the English word Hello.

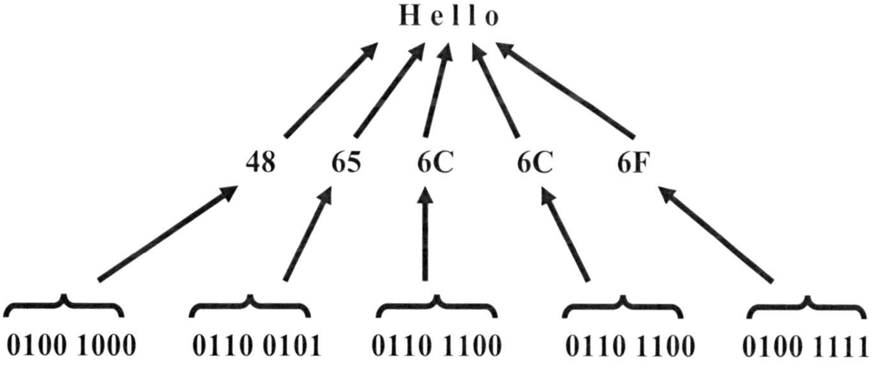

Figure 58

As you study this relationship you will note the individual bits represent the binary equivalents at the lowest level of the computer. Each sting of bits makes up one byte. Each byte is comprised of two nibbles. Considering the numeric place value of each nibble, the first nibble in the furthermost left of the binary string is 0100. This represents the number value of 4 in binary. The next nibble consists of a binary string of 1000. This represents the number value of 8 in binary. Thus, the next level, as interpreted by the operating system shows the 48 in hexadecimal. If you look at your ASCII chart you will discover that a 48 in ASCII is equivalent to the capital letter H. Relate the rest of the binary data sting to the remainder of the characters.

How this is significant to the forensics examiner is that there is an operating system utility called Debug. Debug permits the viewing of hexadecimal information on the disk. Forensics Lab # 5 will introduce how to use debug and how it relates memory contents to characters.

Perform Forensics Lab # 5

TITLE: Understanding Computer Forensics Using Debug

OBJECTIVE:

To become familiar with file structures and how to view them with Debug

Viewing File Structures Using WinHex

WinHex is a hex editing tool that will display the structure of a file in a hexadecimal format, much like the operating system sees it. The benefit of this capability to the forensic examiner is the file headers and file structures of individual files can be displayed. Each file has some method to identify what type of file it is to the operating system. The first several bytes of a file usually provide that identification. This is known as the file header. For example, the header for an executable program will have the characters MZ. A typical Microsoft Office document will have the characters ÐÏ.à¡±.á.

Figure 59 shows a folder of various files. Each of these files contain the same text strings, however, each file was created using a different application or editing tool. Viewing each of these individual files under a hex editing tool such as WinHex will reveal the file structure and header information.

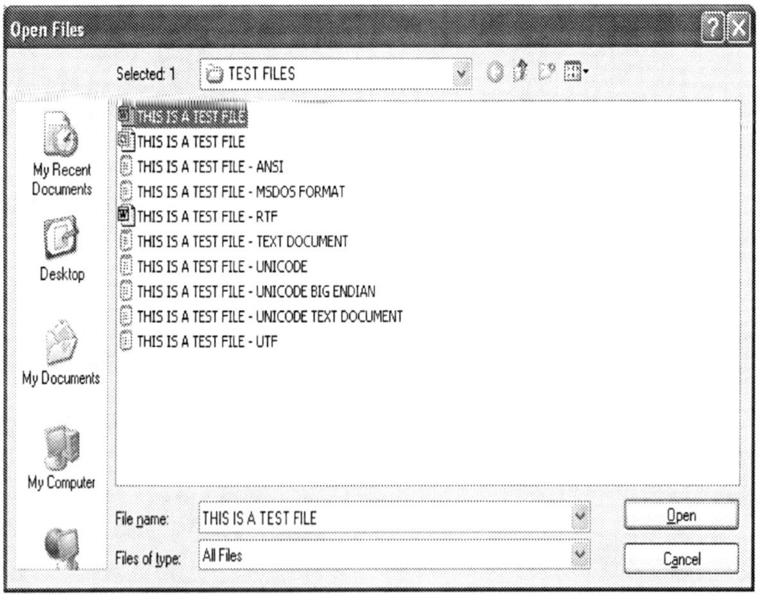

Figure 59

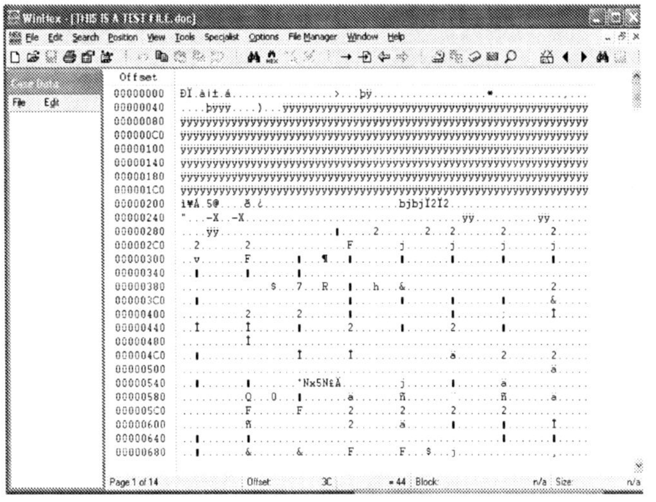

Figure 60

Figure 60 shows the first several bytes of the file, thus, revealing the file header. Note the ÐÏ.à¡±.á characters.

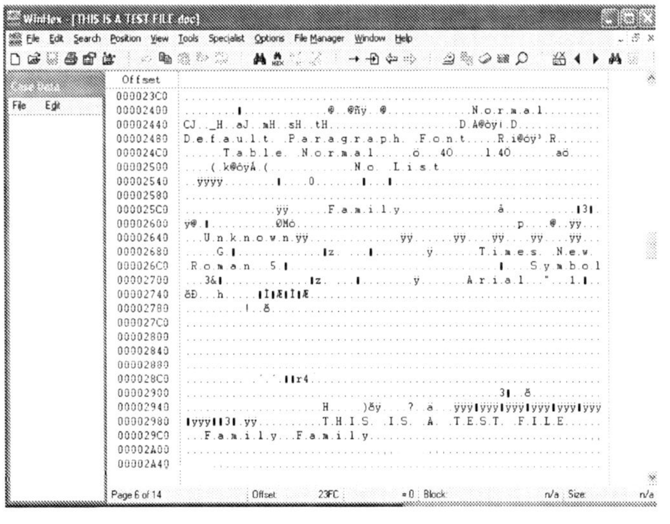

Figure 61

Figures 61 and 62 display information further in the file, thus revealing formatting and font information of the file.

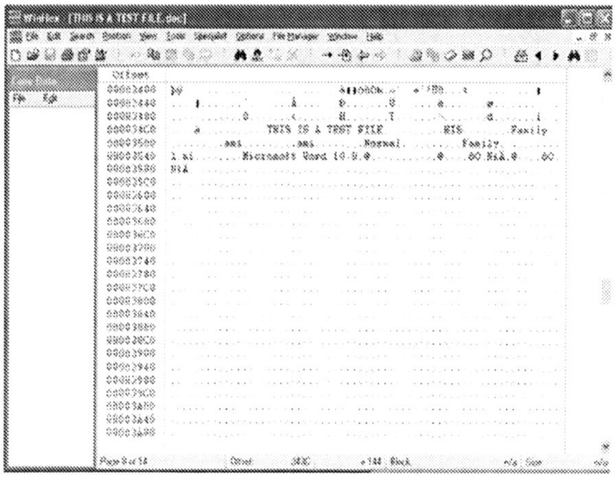

Figure 62

```
00000000  D0 CF 11 E0 A1 B1  1A E1 00 00 00 00 00 00  00 00   ÐÏ.à¡±.á........
00000010  00  00  00 00  00 00  00 00   3E 00 03 00 FE FF 09 00   ........>...þÿ..
00000020  06  00  00 00  00 00  00 00   00 00 00 00 12  00  00 00   ................
00000030  75  08  00 00  00 00  00 00   00 10 00 00 77  08  00 00   u...........w...
00000040  01  00  00 00  FE FF FF FF   00 00 00 00 78  08  00 00   ....þÿÿÿ....x...
00000050  79  08  00 00  7A 08  00 00  7B 08 00 00 7C 08  00 00   y...z...{...|...
00000060  7D 08  00 00  7E 08  00 00   7F 08 00 00 80  08  00 00   }...~...□...€...
00000070  81  08  00 00  82 08  00 00   83 08 00 00 84  08  00 00   □...,...ƒ...„...
00000080  85  08  00 00  86 08  00 00   87 08 00 00 76  08  00 00   ......†...‡...v...
```

This view of a Microsoft Word document shows a string of 00000000 on the left side. This represents the starting address information for that string. The D0 is located in the contents of address 00000000 for this file. The CF is located in address 00000001. The addressing scheme is in hexadecimal, so the 10th memory location contains a 00 and the address is 0000000A.

The fourth line addressing begins with 00000030. Again, this is hexadecimal addressing so the contents of the first memory address on this line is 75. The contents of the 13th memory location is 77. The last memory address on that line is 0000000F and its contents is 00. (If you do not understand binary and hexadecimal numbering systems, stop here and review. Return to this section when you better understand binary and hexadecimal)

```
00000000  D0 CF 11 E0 A1 B1 1A E1 00 00 00 00 00 00 00 00   ÐÏ.à¡±.á...
00000010  00 00 00 00 00 00 00 00 3E 00 03 00 FE FF 09 00   ........>...þÿ..
00000020  06  00  00 00  00 00  00  00 00 00 00 00 12  00 00 00   ................
00000030  75  08  00 00  00 00  00  00 00 10 00 00 77  08 00 00   u...........w...
00000040  01  00  00 00  FE FF FF FF 00 00 00 00 78  08 00 00   ....þÿÿÿ....x...
00000050  79  08 00  00  7A 08 00 00  7B 08 00 00 7C 08 00 00   y...z...{...|...
00000060  7D 08 00  00  7E  08 00 00  7F 08 00 00 80  08 00 00
```

The first line of the file contains the file header, as shown here

Figure 63

This is the file header of an Excel File that has been altered.

```
00000000  00 00 00 00 00 00 00 00  00 00 00 00 00 00 00 00   ................
00000010  00 00 00 00 00 00 00 00  3E 00 03 00 FE FF 09 00   ........>...þÿ..
00000020  06 00 00 00 00 00 00 00  00 00 00 00 01 00 00 00   ................
```

Notice the file header contains all 00's. Although this particular file is still intact as a Microsoft document, it will not be opened by the application that created it because of a corrupted header.

Perform Forensics Lab # 6

TITLE: Floppy Disk Exercise Using WinHex

OBJECTIVE:

To become familiar with how data on a disk can be located by a string search using any hex editing tool, regardless of how the operating system views it.

Perform Forensics Lab # 7

TITLE: Comparing File Structures Using WinHex

OBJECTIVE:

To become familiar with file structures and how to view them with WinHex

Perform Forensics Lab # 8

TITLE: Identifying File Types by Extension

OBJECTIVE:

To become familiar with the large number of file extension types.

Computer Forensics Terms and Definitions

Computer forensics literacy is vital to communicating in this profession. But unlike traditional courses in computer literacy, just knowing the term is not enough, the examiner must understand it. Research each of the following terms and perform forensics lab # 9. You may use a variety of sources, either on-line dictionaries, text books or other materials. Make sure your definitions and explanations are accurate to the field of computer and digital forensics. Providing a description for a worm that lives in the ground and crawls is not the same as a worm that propagates between computer networks and causes malicious destruction of database and files.

Digital Forensic Science	Bit
Byte	Nibble
Cluster	CFCE
ISFA	ISFCE
Policy	Procedure
Guideline	Vulnerability
Evidence	Spyware
Malware	Virus
Trojan Horse	Worm
Platter	Sector
Cylinder	NIST
ILook	MFT
FAT 12	FAT 16
FAT 32	NTFS
HPFS	Metadata
Hash	Message Digest
Digital Signature	Evidence
Steganography	DOJ
IACIS	HTCIA
IISFA	Slack Space
Swap File	On-Track Software

Perform Forensics Lab # 9

TITLE: Computer Forensics Definitions and Terms

OBJECTIVE:

It is necessary that a computer forensic specialist have an understanding of topics and issues collateral to the field. This exercise will provide additional insight into the language of computer forensics and related computer technology.

Creating and Analyzing Disk Images

There are some basic principles associated with the creation of a forensic image file. They are:

1. A forensically sound image is as good as the original
2. A forensically sound image MAY be admissible in court

Acquiring an Image Using Various Tools

There are several tools and methods to acquire a forensically sound image of a disk drive, but all must maintain the same level of integrity with that image. They must not alter it, they must make an exact duplicate of it, and a hashing algorithm should be performed on the acquired image to validate it against the original.

Some of the tools that are or may be used to acquire an image include

1. The Linux dd command
2. The FTK Imager program
3. Safeback imaging program
4. Ghost (bit stream image option only)

It should be noted that perform an image using the Ghost program does not automatically perform a forensically sound bit stream image of the original media. There are software switch options that must be invoked to provide this capability. Before using Ghost or any data or image acquisition tool or program the examiner should review it extensively and practice in a non-critical environment.

Steps in the Forensics Acquisition and Analysis Process

The steps to acquire an image must be sound, verifiable and repeatable. This is to demonstrate reliability and accuracy. In the event that the acquisition and or analysis of the media image is challenged, it can must be able to be demonstrated.

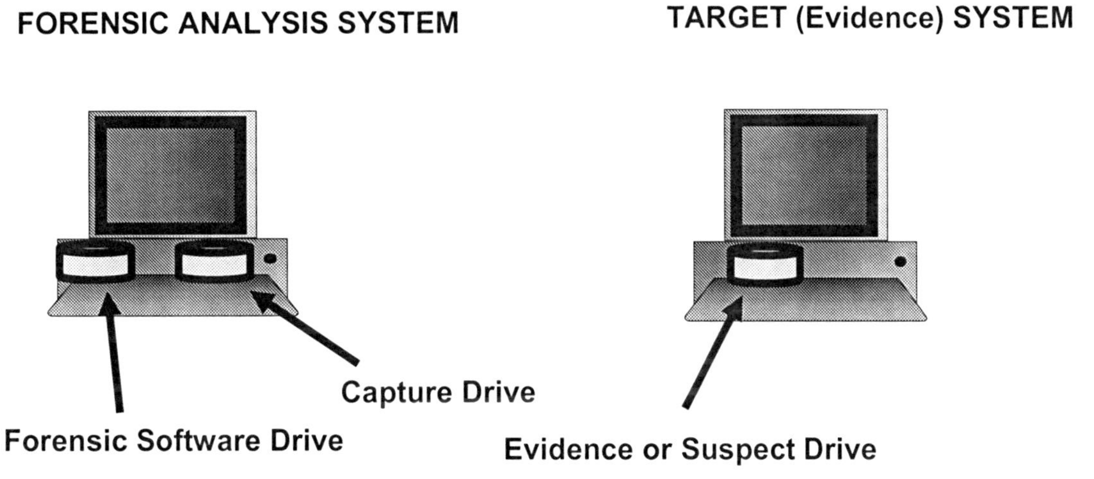

Figure 64

As explained previously, the first step in a forensic analysis is to secure the environment. This includes the local area, the system and the disk drive. This is to prevent any inadvertent or intentional use of the system. Using a system that is desired to be forensically examined will alter the storage environment. Practically every user action on a system can potentially write data to the drive, thus possibly overwriting files.

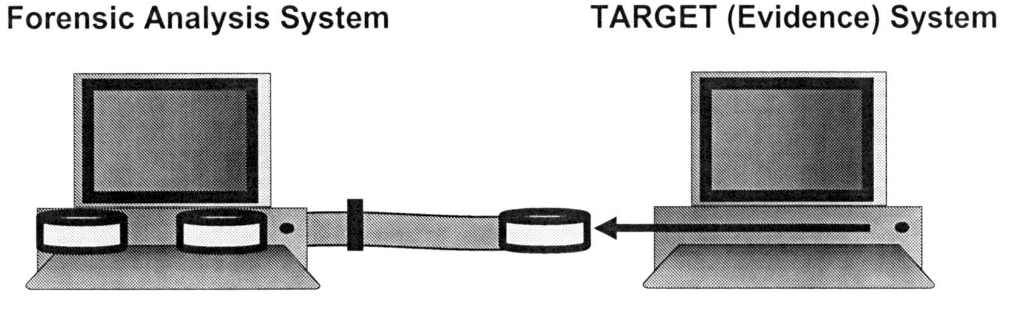

Figure 65

The next step is, after the environment has been secured, the evidence or target drive should be removed and placed in a forensic recovery system for duplication of the drive image.

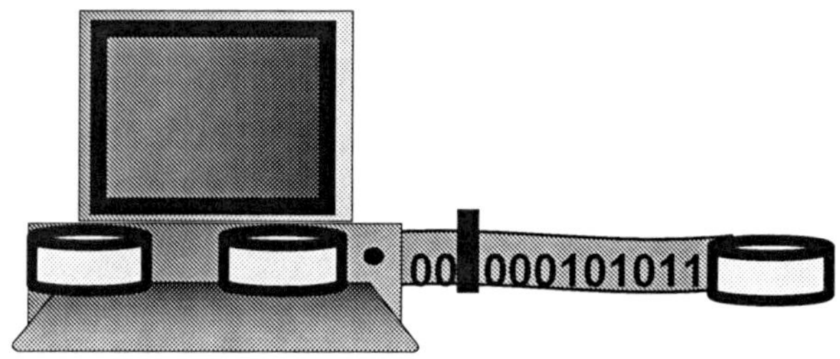

Figure 66

Once the drive has been inserted into the system an image can be acquired

After the acquisition has been achieved, the drive should be stored in a secure location and the chain-of-custody documentation updated to reflect proper handling and storage.

Figure 67

FORENSIC ANALYSIS SYSTEM

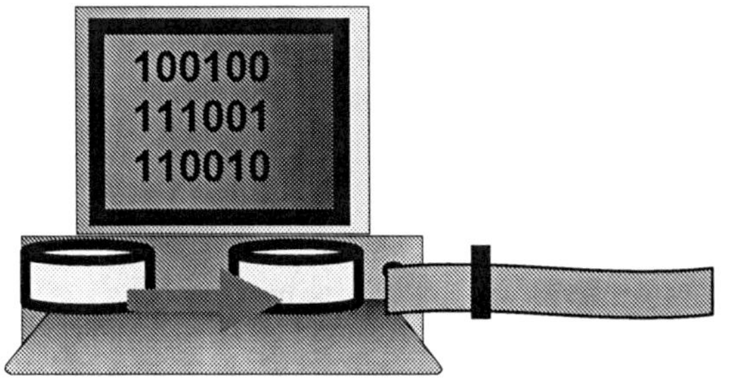

Figure 68

Once the image has been acquired and the evidence or target drive has been secured, the drive image can be analyzed.

The final step of the process is to create the necessary or desired documentation.

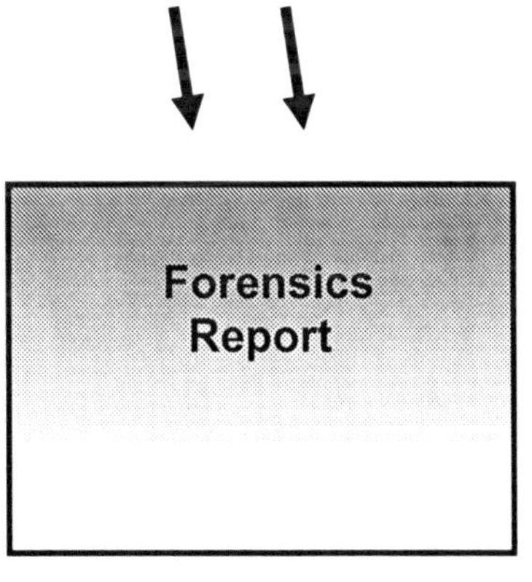

Figure 69

As a reminder, it must be noted that an acquired image of a disk drive, if validated with a recognized hashing algorithm such as SHA-1 or MD5, is considered as valid as the original or source media.

Acquiring the Image Using FTK

To create a valid bit stream image of a source media, several precautions must be taken. Perhaps the most important is that of ensuring that the original is not corrupted and the copy is an exact duplicate. The write blocker is vital in providing this level of confidence.

To create an image of a source media using the Access Data FTK program,

1. Click on the FTK Imager.lnk logo.

Figure 70

The FTK Imager window should appear.

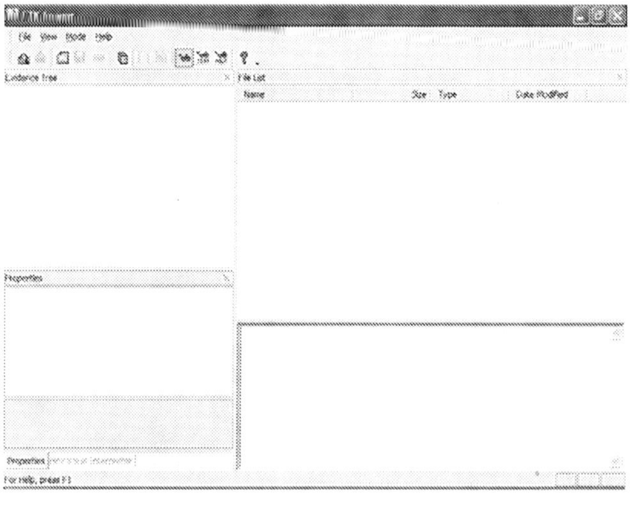

Figure 71

2. Next select the File pull down window and click on Create Disk Image.

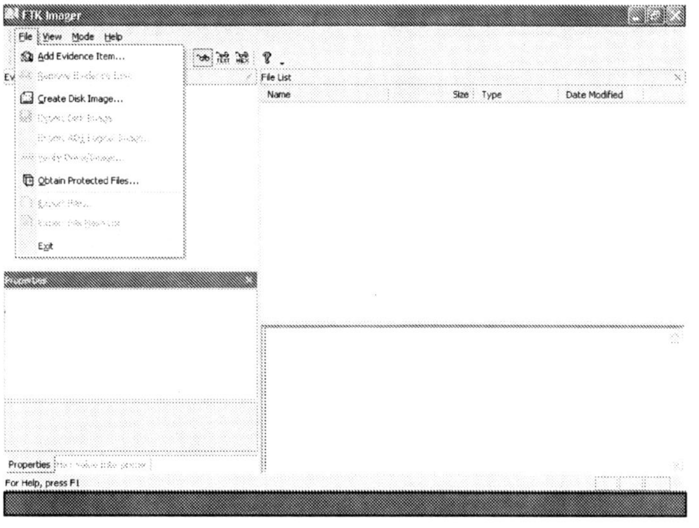

Figure 72

You should then be presented with the Select Source window. This window provides multiple options for acquiring and creating an image file.

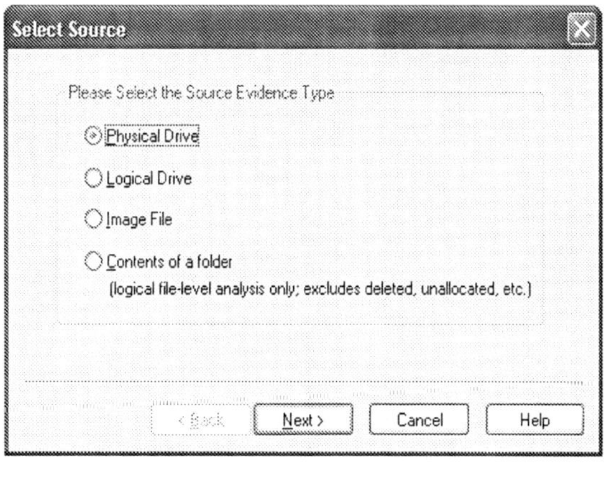

Figure 73

The Physical Drive option will acquire an image of the entire media, regardless of partition information or logical drive letters or assignment. This will capture even unpartitioned drive space.

The Logical Drive option will acquire and create an image file of a logical drive and not the entire physical drive. Selecting this option will not acquire data or bit streams from other parts of the drive.

The Image File option will acquire an already created image file.

The Contents of a Folder option will acquire all data and files within a specified folder on the hard disk. This includes deleted files or information that may be within the boundary of the folder start and end addresses.

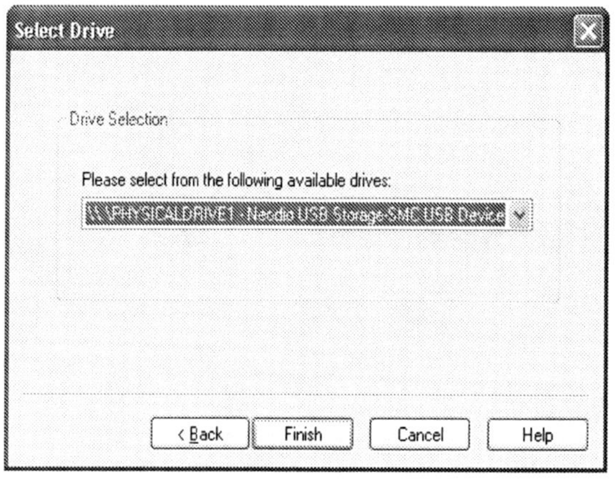

Figure 74

The next window that will appear will be the Select Drive window. This is where the examiner identifies which device to acquire the image file from.

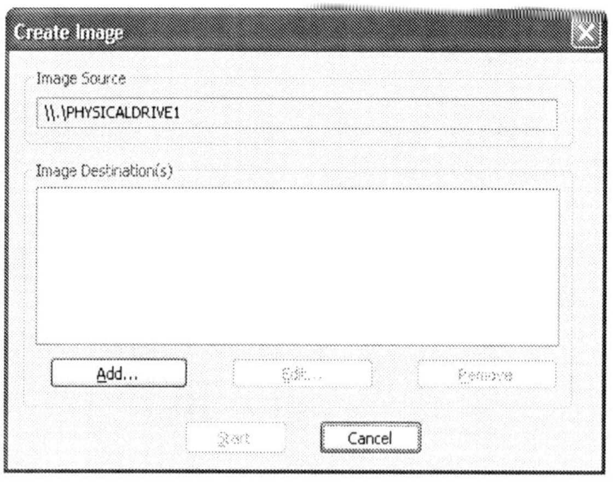

Figure 75

The Create Image window will appear. At this point the forensic examiner will click the Add button to add the image file to the acquisition process.

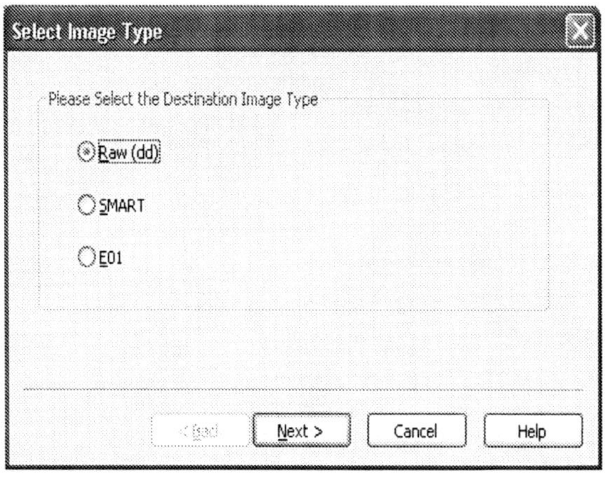

Figure 76

The Select Image Type window is where the specific type of image file to be created is selected.

The RAW option will make acquire and create an exact bit by bit replica of the source media.

The Smart option will compress the image file.

The E01 option will crate an image file that is compatible with Encase analysis software.

Each of these options provides a hash value output that is compared against the original media hash value. Thus, all options are considered forensically sound.

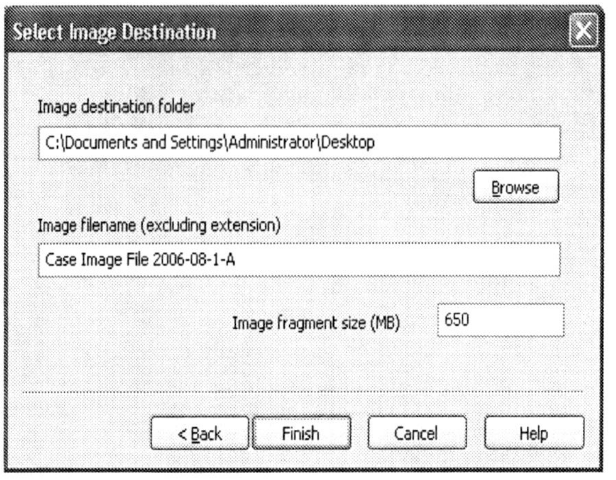

Figure 77

The Select Image Destination window provides the opportunity to determine the Image destination folder and the Image filename. The forensic examiner should have an established naming convention for case image files. One suggestion is that case image files be identified by date and perhaps client name. For example, a case image file that is created on June 1st, 2007 and is associated with the Smith account, it might be labeled Case 2007-6-01-Smith.

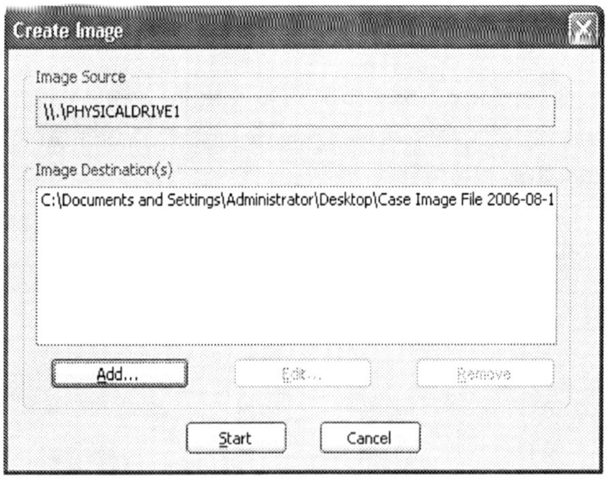

Figure 78

The Create Image window then reappears and present the path information to the examiner for confirmation. Once the examiner selects the Start button, the drive acquisition and image file creation process begins.

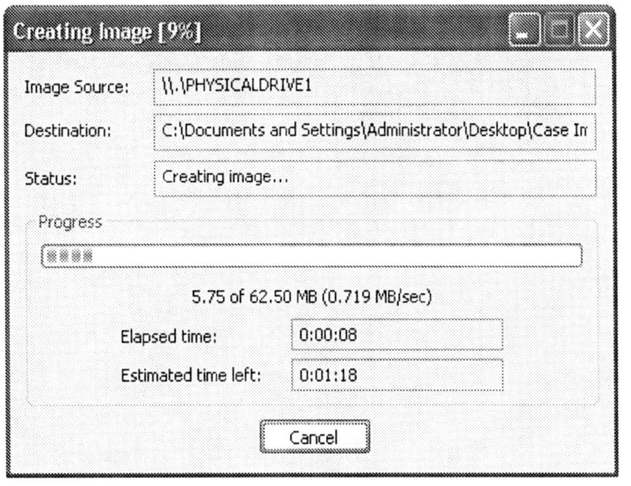

Figure 79

As the image file is being created a status or Progress line is visible. The time for an image is dependent upon the following factors.

1. Size of the media being imaged
2. Speed of the interface with the media
3. Speed of the system bus of the forensic analysis system

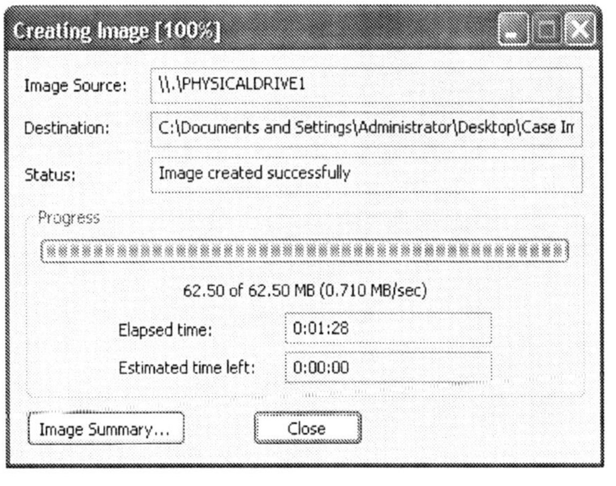

Figure 80

Once completed the Image Summary option becomes available. This option will provide status as to the parameters of the acquisition.

Figure 81

The Image summary file is then provided next to the actual created bit stream image file. (Figure 82)

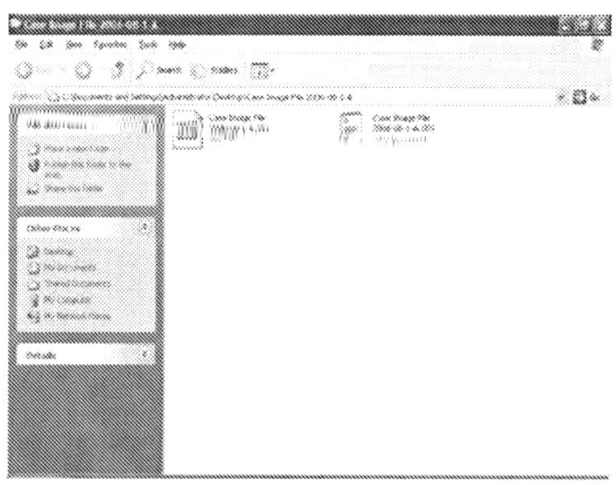

Figure 82

Figure 83

Figure 83 shows the provided text file with specifics of the image including hash values, drive geometry, drive model and interface type. This information must be correlated to the forensic reporting documentation, the chain-of-custody and receipt information. This will minimize or eliminate misunderstanding as to which drive was imaged and analyzed.

Perform Forensics Lab # 10

TITLE: FTK Imaging

OBJECTIVE:

To acquire an image of a target media using the FTK Imager program.

Analyzing Images Using FTK

Once the image has been properly acquired, it may be analyzed. These steps are demonstrated using the Access Data FTK program.

1. Initialize the FTK application

Figure 84

If your FTK program is not utilizing the KFF Library, you should receive this error message.

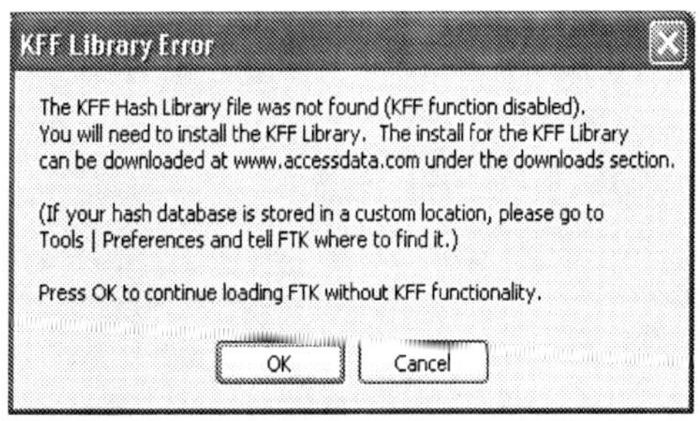

Figure 85

KFF stands for Known File Filter and is a database of hash values for known existing operating system files. Being the many thousands of files comprise the Windows operating system, each one of these files has had a hash calculation performed on it and the results stored in this database. The purpose of this is to eliminate any known hash values from the analysis phase. Thus, saving the forensic examiner many hundreds of hours of time sifting through unnecessary files.

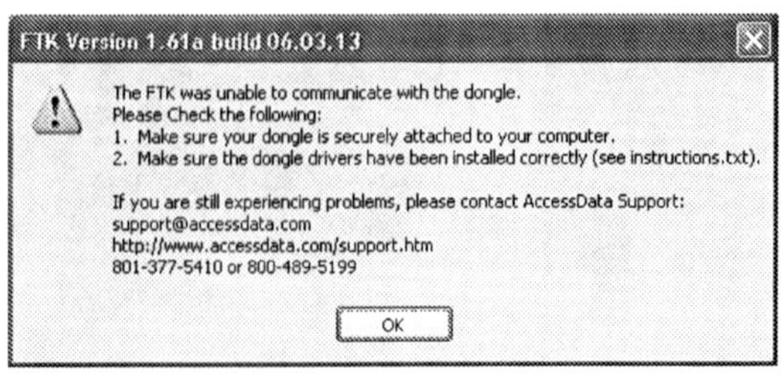

Figure 86

If you are using the demo version of FTK, you will receive this message as well. It is reporting that the software did not authenticate to the dongle. The dongle is necessary for the FTK program to have full functionality with an entire operating system. Without the dongle, FTK is limited to processing up to 5000 files. Most operating systems have many more files than this. This is OK with this forensic training program as the case image files used are under the 5000 file limitation of the demo software.

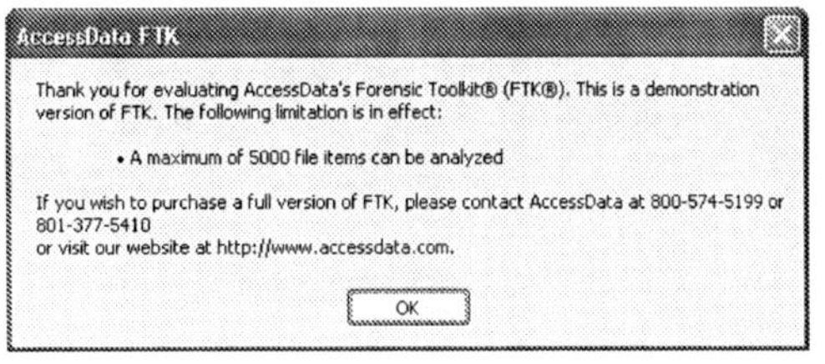

Figure 87

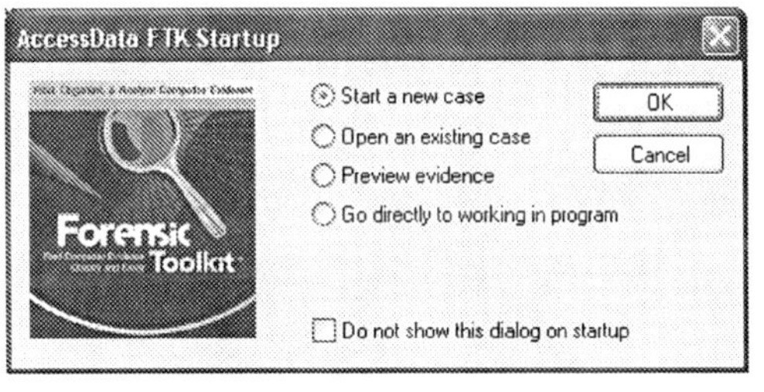

Figure 88

The AccessData FTK Startup window will then appear providing the options as listed. Since this is your first time using FTK with this program, you will select the Start a new case option.

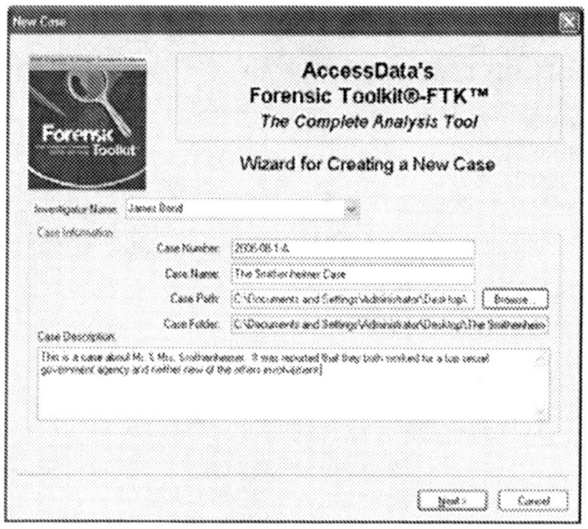

Figure 89

The next option you will be presented requires you to complete the case information. This information is vital to efficient and accurate analysis and reporting and the examiner will not be permitted to advance past this window until the necessary information is provided. The information from this and the next steps is recorded in the FTK folder that will be created as a result of analyzing the image file.

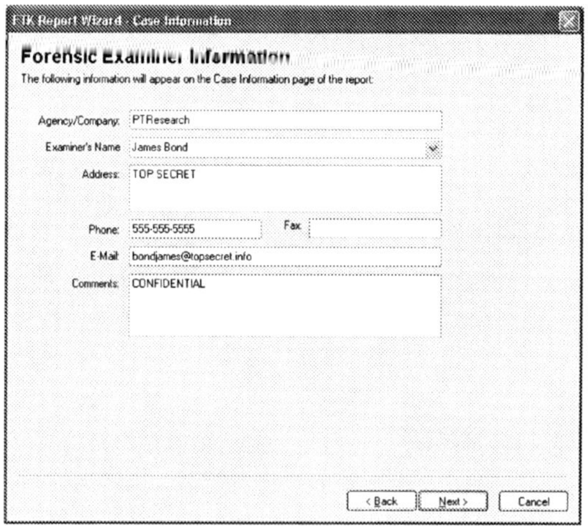

Figure 90

The next window also requires examiner information and will be included in the case image folder that will be created.

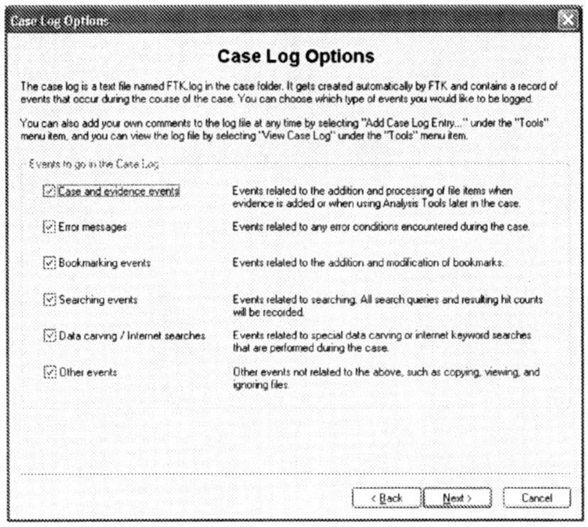

Figure 91

The Case Log Options window will appear and provides the examiner several options. Descriptions of each option is provided in this window. It is usually best to select all options at this window.

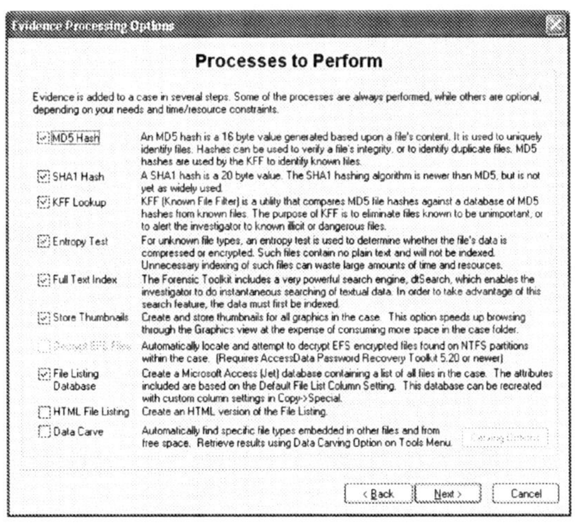

Figure 92

The Processes to Perform window provide the examiner with the options to be performed by FTK during the indexing phase. Again, the descriptions of each option are identified in this window.

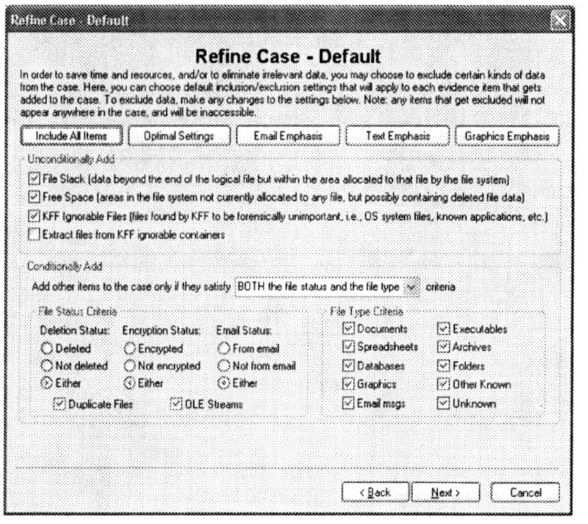

Figure 93

The Refine Case – Default window provides the option of selecting or deselecting certain file types for processing and identification of this case image file. Unless the examiner desires to recover a specific type of file, the defaults are generally all applied.

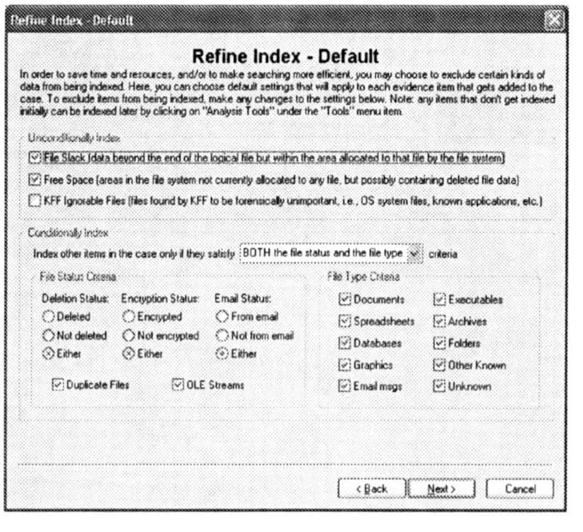

Figure 94

The Refine Index – Default window provides the options of how to process or treat the files within the image.

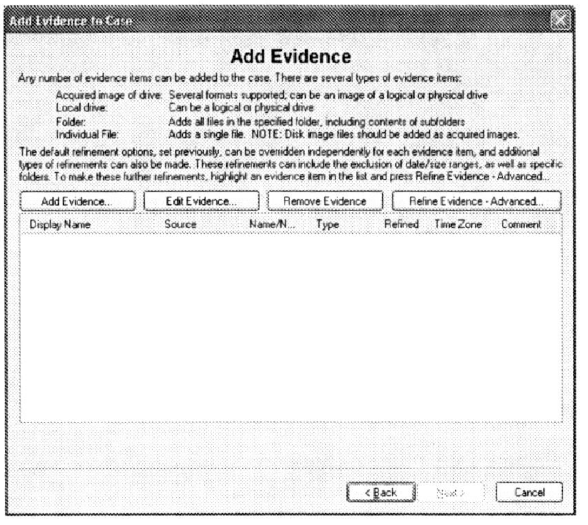

Figure 95

The Add Evidence window is where the examiner selects the particular case image file to be processed by FTK. A forensic examiner may have dozens or hundreds of case image files and it is imperative that the correct image file be added and processed by FTK. This is where the importance of identifying the created image file b an efficient naming convention is as critical.

At this point in the forensic set up process, the examiner would click on the Add Evidence button. This will open the following window.

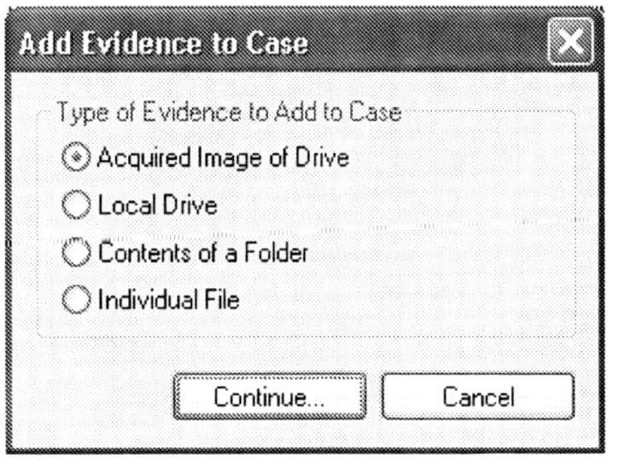

Figure 96

This window permits selection of the case image file. At this point, the examiner would select the Acquired Image of Drive radial button.

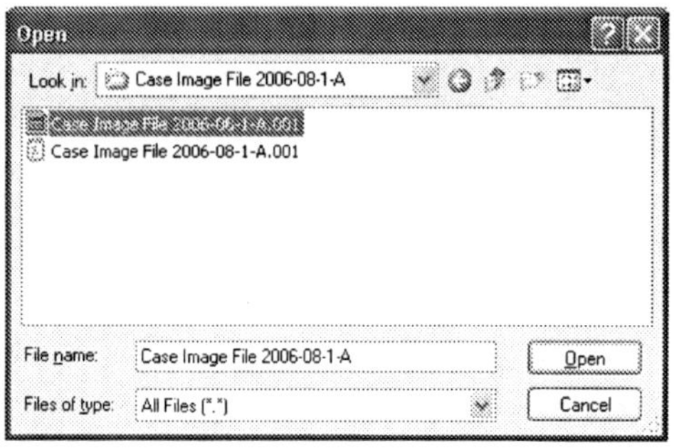

Figure 97

The examiner then would navigate to the location of the case image file. Note that two files are present within the case image folder. One is a text file that has the acquisition parameters recorded. The other is the case image file. The case image file is the file to be selected and the Open button clicked.

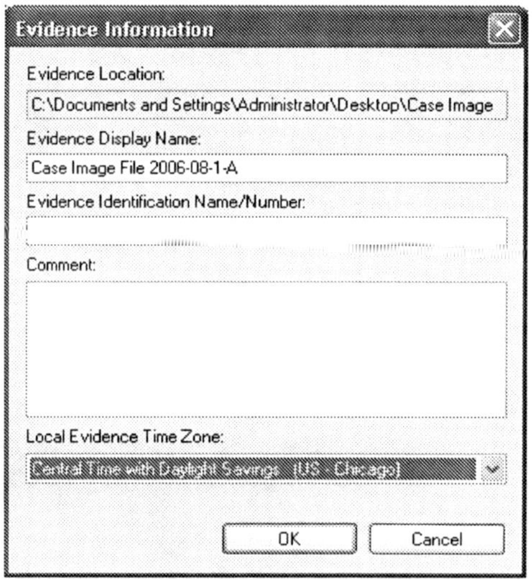

Figure 98

After the case image file has been selected for loading into FTK, the Evidence Information window appears. The location of the evidence file and name is verified at this point. Again, FTK will not permit the examiner to proceed until the time zone is selected. It is common practice to select the time zone the drive was imaged in.

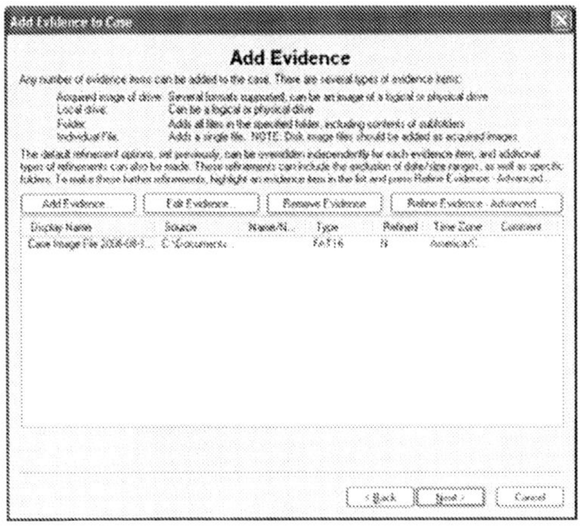

Figure 99

The Add Evidence window appears confirming the case image file to be processed. At this point the examiner clicks the Next button.

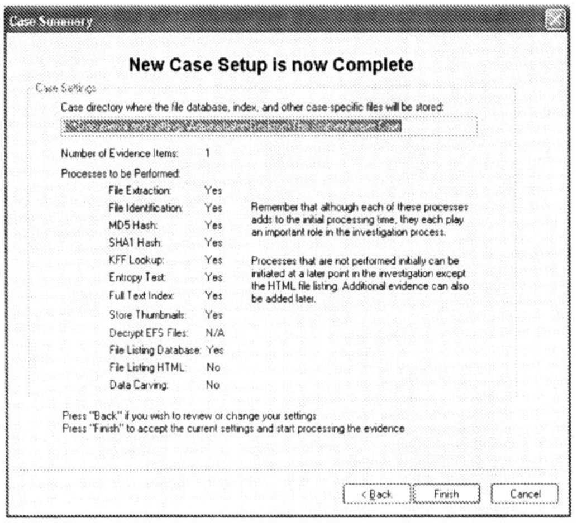

Figure 100

The New Case Setup window appears and confirms the examiner options. Clicking Finish will begin processing and indexing of the image file.

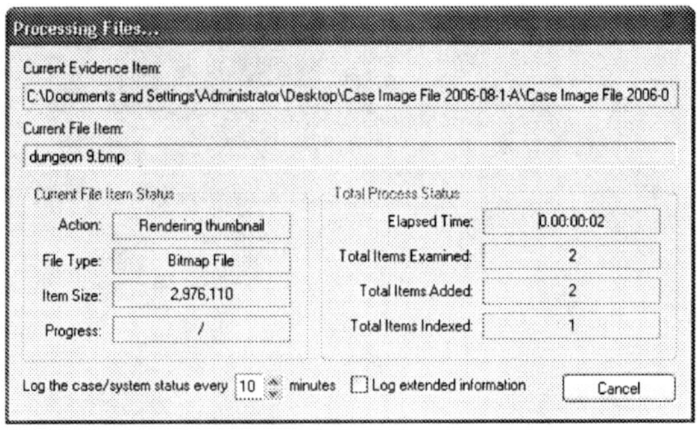

Figure 101

Where the previous steps may take only a matter of minutes, this step may take many hours. Some cases, depending upon the size of the hard disk, may take ten or more hours. This window provides status as to the current actions taking place in the processing and indexing of the case image file. The elapsed time is also presented.

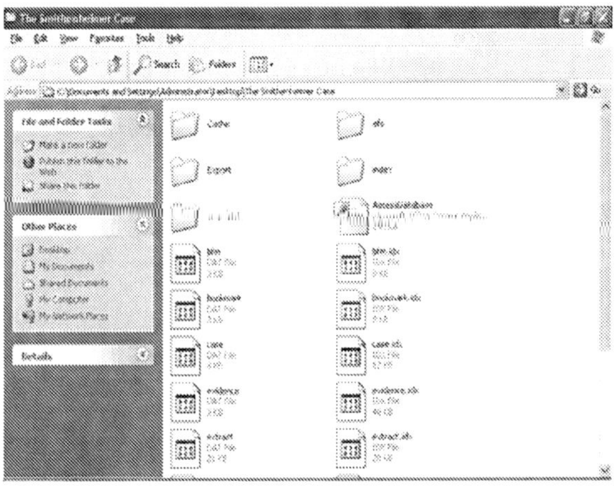

Figure 102

The results of FTK processing an image file is that all of the identifiable contents of that image file have been identified and categorized by type, and much of the contents of the image such as intact files have had a hash calculation performed on them.

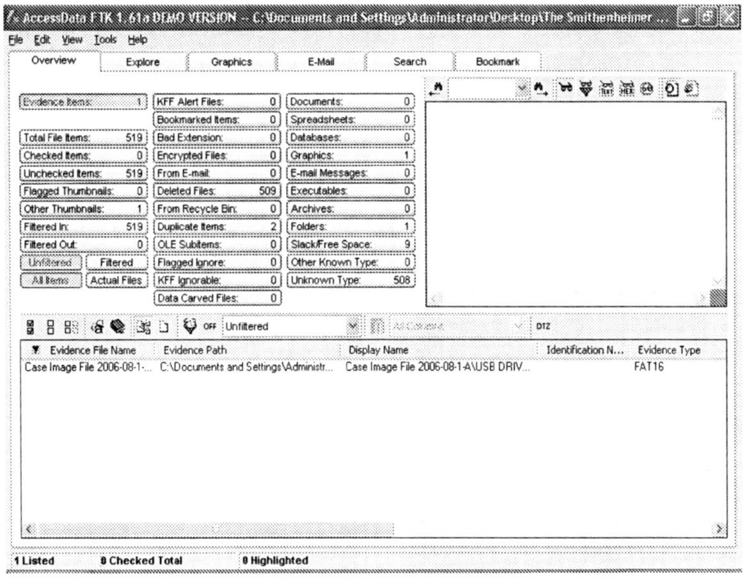

Figure 103

The FTK program will display the case as identified and processed. To view identified graphic files, click the Graphics tab. To view identified encrypted documents, click the Encrypted Files button.

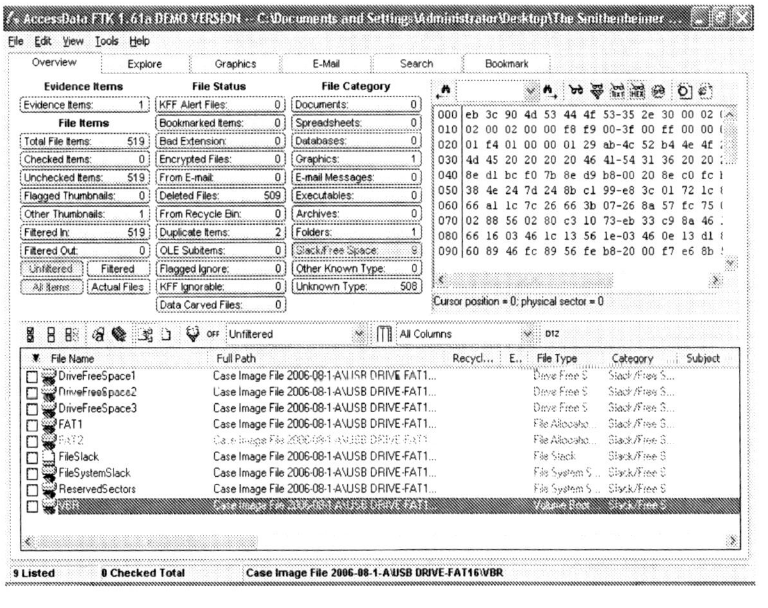

Figure 104

The examiner may then navigate throughout the image file. At this point, the intuitiveness and skill of the examiner is most critical. Where many files are simple text or executable files, some may contain steganography or be encrypted. Depending upon the emphasis of the examination, the examiner may look only for a single file or type of file to recover, or examine an entire drive for compliance to a defined security policy or law.

One aspect of evaluating a disk drive is to let the image provide the questions as well as the answers. Since the created image has been bit streamed into an organized and categorized image file. Thus, all data strings are listed in alphabetical order as an option under FTK. By reviewing these data strings, many interesting words appear. Using these words the examiner can search their context within the image.

The filtering process of a disk image involves the processing of certain types of space from the drive. There are three primary areas that provide data or information regarding use of the system. They are swap data, slack data and free or unallocated space. These areas are outside of typical user access and result from the normal activities of the operating system. From these areas, keywords can be identified and used in combination with other keywords to possibly reveal related sentences or text.

For example, if the word "drugs" appeared, the examiner could select the word and under FTK, navigate to all of the places in the image that that word appeared. The word "drugs" may be found in a text document describing a medical procedure, or a saved web page on how to treat poison ivy. Using the combination of the words "password" and "e-mail" may or may not yield a password to an e-mail account.

The examiner must be very careful during this phase so as not to draw conclusions or present an image of user intentions. Finding the word "drugs" does not infer criminal wrongdoing. The job of the forensic examiner is to discover and report their findings, not to conclude user intentions. If the examination involves a legal or criminal situation, the examiner is to provide the facts and let those with legal authority make any determinations. The corporate computer examiner should always remember that they are not law enforcement and are subject to the same guidelines as others.

Drive Image Text Processing

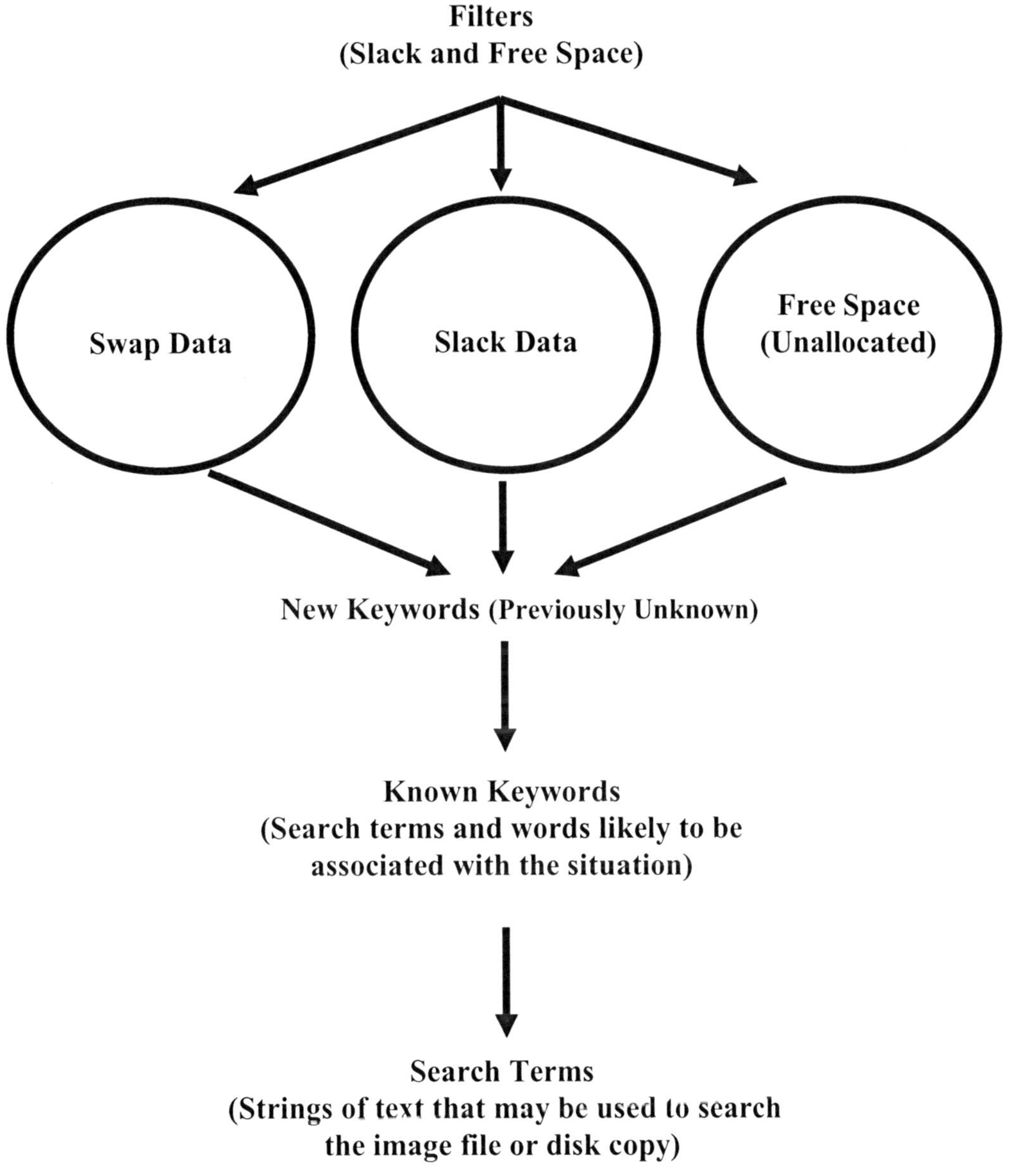

Figure 105

Perform Forensics Lab # 11

TITLE: Analyze an Acquired Image File Using FTK (Case Image file 2005-10)

OBJECTIVE:

To analyze a particular media to determine if any information of evidentiary value is contained within and to report on it.

Perform Forensics Lab # 12

TITLE: Analyze an Image File Using FTK (Case Image file 2005-20)

OBJECTIVE:

To analyze a particular media to determine if any information of evidentiary value is contained within and to report on it.

Text files can not be modified under forensic analysis. To do so would invalidate the integrity of the examination. After a particular file of interest has been identified, it can be exported outside of the image for further analysis. To export a file, right click on that file and select Export File.

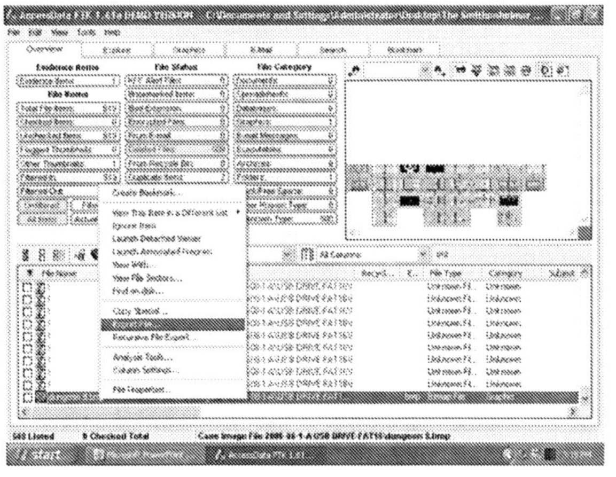

Figure 106

The export path will be identified. Note that more than one file may be exported by selecting the check box next to it as show above.

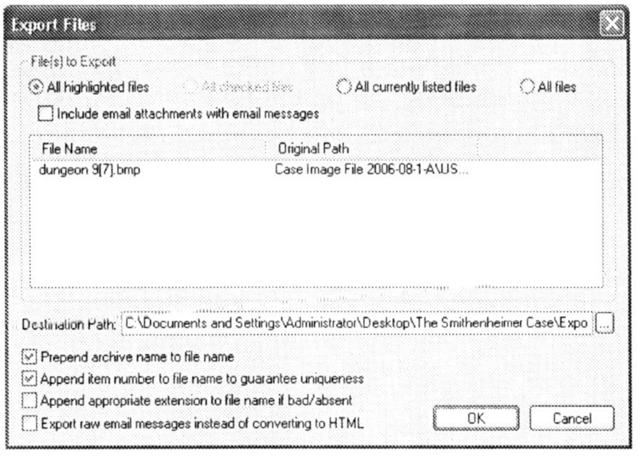

Figure 107

Once successfully exported, the Export Files window will appear.

Figure 108

At this point the file may be examined as it would be under normal operating system conditions.

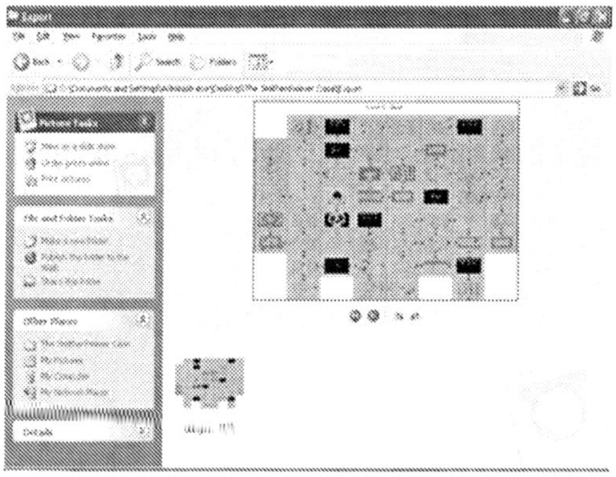

Figure 109

If the exported file is password protected (encrypted), the password must be found to reconstruct the file back to its native format. FTK will identify encrypted files within the image but they must be exported to be recovered.

Selecting your password recovery tool of choice is the next step.

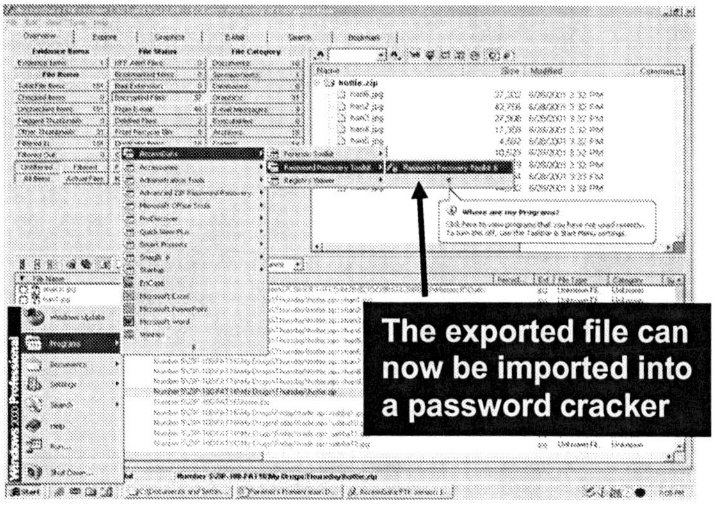

Figure 110

Excel File Recovery and Reconstruction

Some exported files may not be executable by the program that created them. This may be due to various reasons, including intentional alteration of the file header in attempts to conceal the file contents, the file may be partially overwritten, or it may be a discontinous file.

Sometimes the file headers are corrupted by partial overwrites and sometimes the file headers are intentionally altered by more experienced users. Minor alterations to a file header can keep the file intact but not permit it to be opened by the native program. This can have the appearance of a viable file but the operating system or native application can not open it. Most users might consider this a corrupted file that is unrecoverable. Figure 111 shows a view of a Microsoft document using the WinHex program.

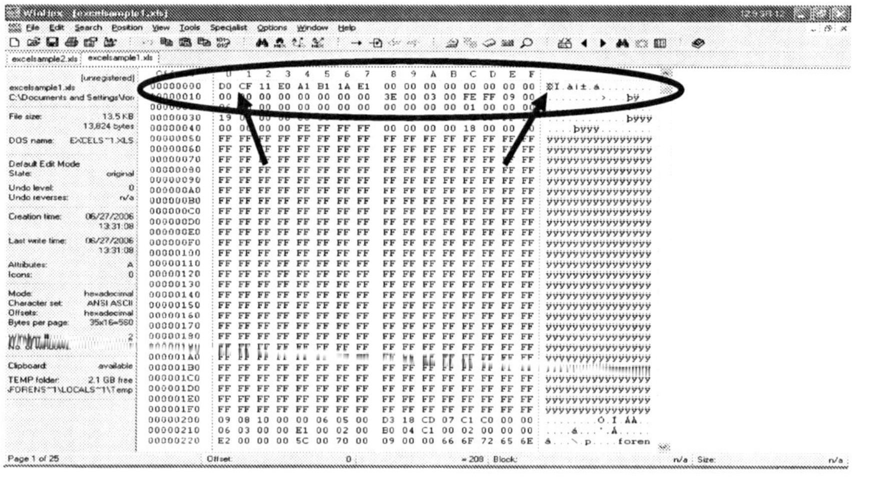

Figure 111

The area identified above includes the file header. The first three bytes of the file are consistent with a Microsoft document. If these three bytes of information are altered, the file will still be displayed as a Microsoft document but will not be opened correctly. See figure 112.

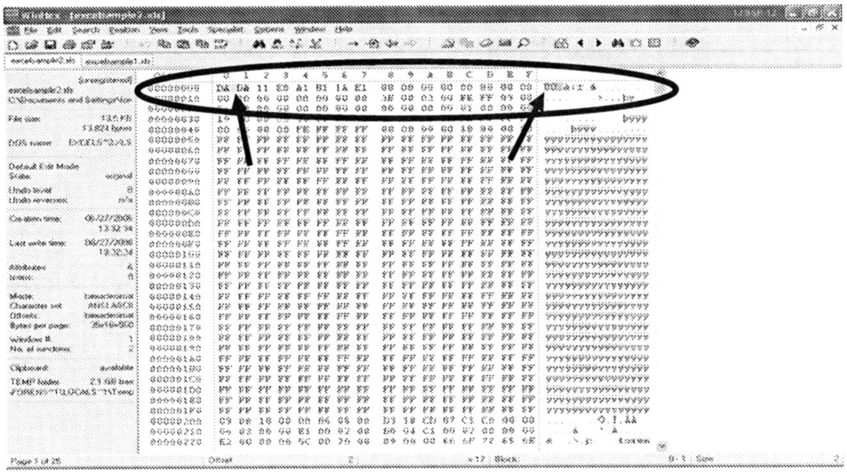

Figure 112

If this is the level and method of file corruption, there are two quick ways to recover the file. One approach is to create another file using the same type of program, and then view the header of that new file. Then, the examiner can reconstruct the file using the new file as a temple.

For example, if the corrupted file is an Excel file, create a new Excel file. Then view this file using WinHex and note the construction of the file header. Then open the corrupted or altered file using WinHex and change the file header to the same values as the new, uncorrupted file.

Some may argue this is not forensically sound but in fact it is. Work is not being performed on the original file, only a copy of it, and it has been reconstructed to a recoverable state. As long as these steps are repeatable and can be validated, your steps are sound.

The other method is to drop the corrupted file into a file recovery program such as the Recovery for Excel application. If the file header is corrupted, this application should be able to reconstruct it. It should be noted that an effective computer examiner can perform this same procedure without the use of automated tools and may need to explain or describe this process to other less technical personnel.

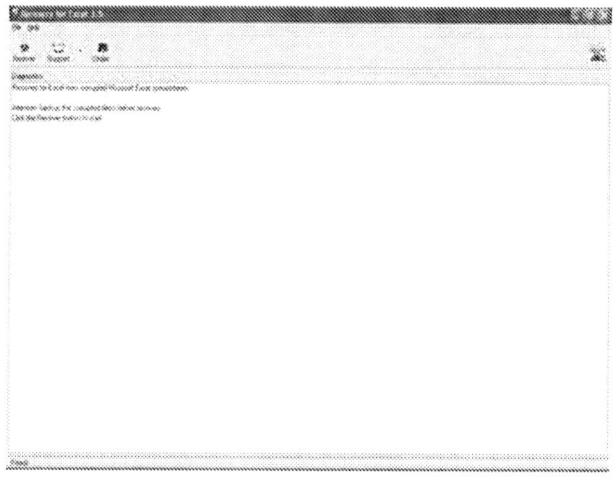

Figure 113

Figure 113 shows the Recovery for Excel window. At this point the examiner can drag and drop the corrupted Excel file into the recovery window.

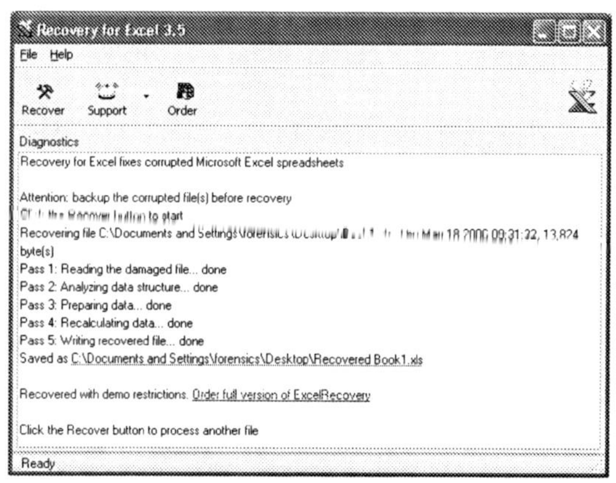

Figure 114

Figure 114 shows the recovery in process. It should be noted that not all corrupted files are easily recovered.

Perform Forensics Lab # 13

TITLE: Reconstruct Damaged or Corrupted Excel Files

OBJECTIVE:

Try to recovery damaged or corrupted Excel files using both manual recovery and automated tools.

Password Policies

As the examiner recovers passwords, they appreciate that an efficient and enforced password policy is critical to the security of the network and the contents of each individual file in that network. The most secure network in the world can be compromised if the authentication to that network has been compromised.

The strength of a password is often taken for granted by users. This is why an effective audit and enforcement policy is vital. And effective password policy will include the following components:

1. Overview
2. Purpose
3. Scope
4. Structure / body of the policy
5. The actual policy itself
6. Enforcement
7. Definitions
8. Revision history
9. Current revision

One example of an effective password policy is presented in the next several pages.

Information Security Policy

Password Policy

1.0 Overview

Passwords are an important part of computer and company security. Without passwords, all data held by this company would be available and visible to anyone and everyone with access to our internal network. Passwords are a first defense against information leaks, and a poorly constructed password, while easy for the user to remember, is also easy for an attacker to guess or break, resulting in compromised data throughout the entire corporation.

Therefore, it is a requirement for all company employees (including outside contractors and any other personnel with workstation access inside the company) to follow the outlined policy below to create passwords that are as secure as possible, and easy for users to remember.

2.0 Purpose

The purpose of this policy is to establish a common policy for creating, securing, changing, and maintaining secure passwords.

3.0 Scope

This document pertains to all company personnel, including all salaried and hourly positions, external contractors with access to any company workstation or other personnel who have access to user accounts on any workstation that resides inside the company or any workstation that has access to or stores non-public information.

4.0 Policy-

4.1 General

Passwords must:

- Be 8 characters minimum length.
- Have 2 upper case characters.
- Have at least 1 special character.
- Have at least 1 numeric character.
- Not contain or be a dictionary word or term.
- Not be written down or stored on any workstation.
- Be changed every 60 days.

4.2 Password Expiration

You will be notified by your workstation when your password is about to expire. While you will be warned up to 2 weeks before password expiration, you will still be able to use that password until expiration. When your password expires, you will not be able to log in until you select a new secure password as outlined by this policy.

4.3 User Accounts

Users will be issued an account as required. Access to all company information, domain services and resources will be obtained through user accounts. Users may only be logged in on one workstation at a time. User accounts will be assigned privileges and be part of an appropriate group with appropriate group permissions. Permissions will be based upon several factors, including data classification.

4.4 General Password Creation Guidelines

Passwords are used for various purposes at Our Company, Inc, these purposes include user-level access, remote access, web access, data and database access, email account logins, local hardware access, and voicemail. Passwords need to be as secure as possible to prevent data from being accessed by anyone other than persons needing to view and edit it.

4.5 Poor Password Elements

- Less than 8 characters in length
- Is or contains a dictionary word or term
- Password is or contains easily guessed everyday use phrases, such as:
    - Name of family members, pets, friends or the like
    - Blank Passwords
    - Important Dates in your life, such as birthdays and anniversaries
    - Company Name or any derivation resembling Company Name
    - Phone Numbers and Addresses
    - Characters with a pattern, such as "aabbcc", "a1b2c3"
    - Appending numbers to the end of dictionary terms, such as "password1"
    - Preceding Dictionary Terms with numbers, such as "1password"
    - Any of the previous spelled backwards

4.6 Strong Password Elements

- At least 8 characters in length
- Contain Upper and Lowercase Letters
- Contain Special Characters, including "!@#$%^&*()"
- Can NOT be identified as a word or slang term in any dictionary, in any language
- Strong passwords should NEVER be written down in desk drawers, under keyboards, on monitors, given out or spoken out loud.
- Passwords should NEVER be stored electronically in any form, under ANY circumstances.

5.0 Passphrase Security

Passphrases are most commonly used for public/private key authentication between two or more persons. It is a method of encrypting data with a private key, so that only persons with the public key may view the information. Passphrases are not like passwords. Passphrases are generally a series of dictionary terms combined with special characters to create the phrase.

Good passphrases are generally fairly long, combining several dictionary terms, upper and lowercase letters, number, and special characters. An example of a good passphrase is "TheWeather|@$tWeekW@$A1!".

6.0 Password Protection

Passwords should never be given out, under any circumstances, to any person. If someone requests your password, refer them to management, this document, or the Information Security Department. Passwords, as stated above, should never be written down, or stored in any electronic form on any workstation or Home PC.

If you suspect that your password has been compromised, notify the Information Security Department immediately.
Password and passphrase examples used in this document are for demonstration only, and are NOT to be used as user level passwords. They are included in this document as a starting point for a secure password or passphrase.

7.0 Policy Enforcement

Any personnel found violating this policy will be subject to disciplinary action, following company guidelines, up to and including termination of employment.

8.0 Definitions

9.0 Revision History

Approved by: **Date:**

______________________________ ____________________

Signed Name: **Date:**

______________________________ ____________________

File Password Recovery

There are multiple tools available for password recovery. One such tool, the Password Recovery Toolkit, is provided with the Access Data Forensics Tool Kit.

Figure 105

The Password Recovery Toolkit can perform the following functions:

- Brute force password protected files
- Dictionary attack password protected files
- Create a dictionary file from an organized word list of the evidence drive

To initialize the Password Recovery Toolkit, click on the Password Recovery Toolkit link. The following window should appear.

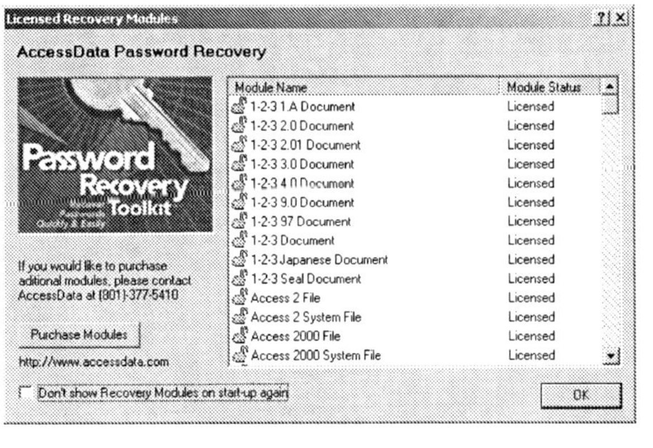

Figure 106

At this point you select the type of file recovery you wish to perform and import the selected file to be recovered.

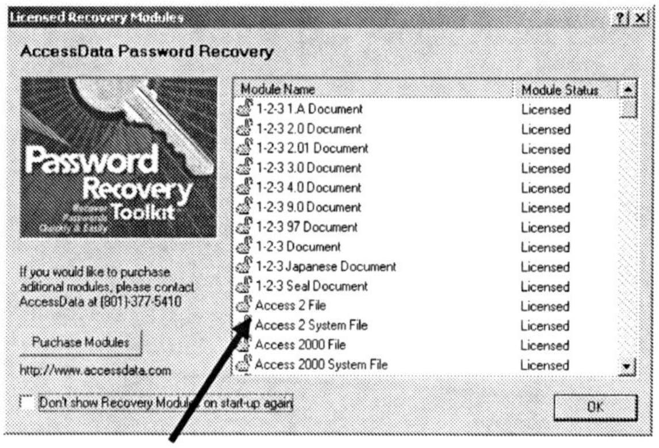

Figure 107

Select the specific type of cracking application

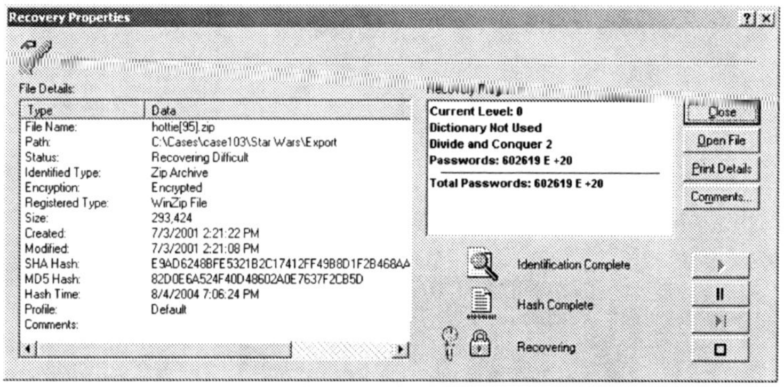

Figure 108

The password cracking operation begins

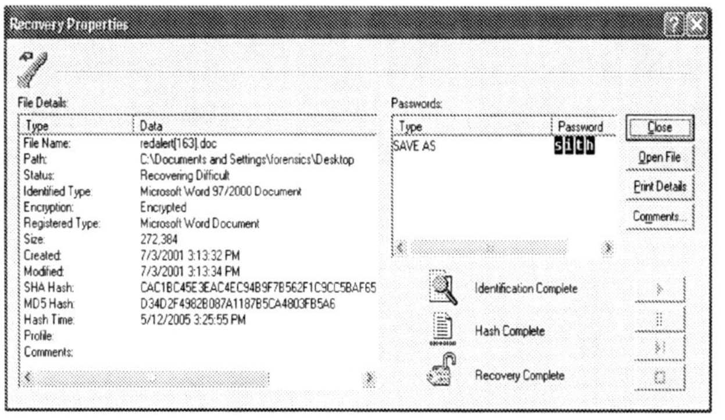

Figure 109

Once the password has been recovered it will be displayed in the Passwords window. This may take a matter of seconds, hours, days, weeks, months or even years, depending upon how complex and efficient the password is.

Another type of password recovery program is the Microsoft Office File Password Recovery tool.

Microsoft Office File Password Recovery

Figure 110

Initialize the Microsoft Office File Password Recovery program and configure the recovery settings.

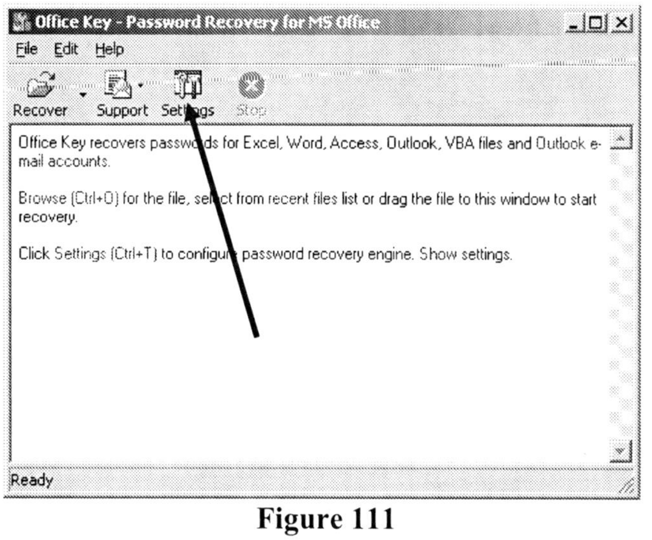

Figure 111

This is an important step as the type of password recovery technique is dependent upon the possible construction of the password. A password consisting of only a couple of characters would best be approached with a brute force attack. A password consisting of six, eight or more characters might best be approached with a dictionary attack first, then followed by a brute force attack.

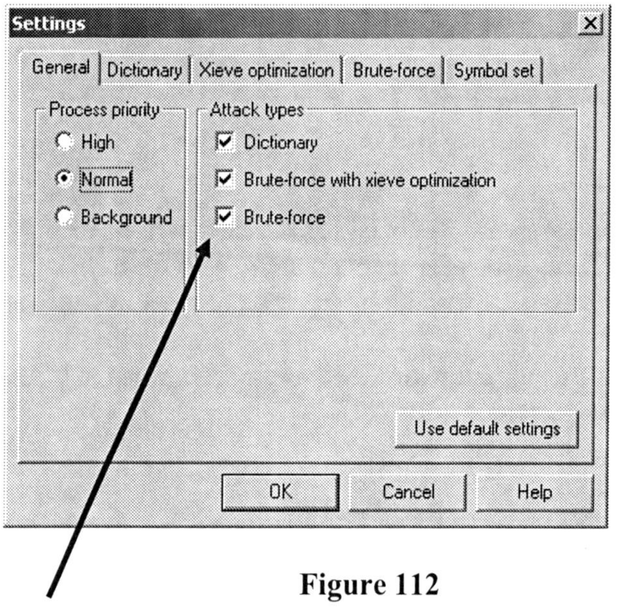

Figure 112

This window provides the cracking options (Attack types).

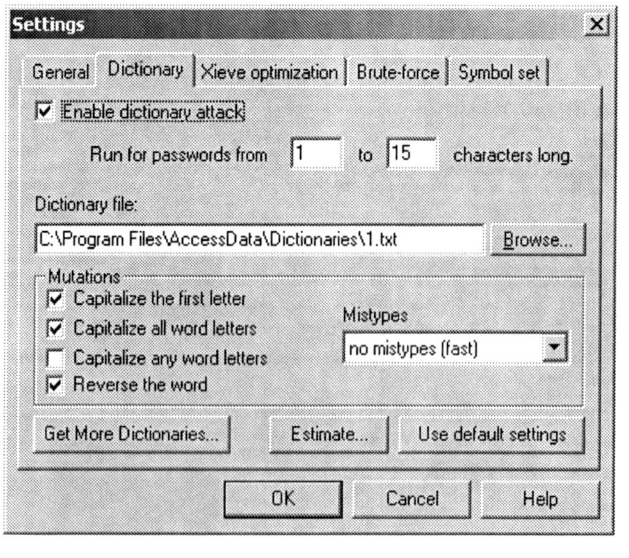

Figure 113

The dictionary attack option (Figure 113) will permit the user to select a dictionary file to be used as a text reference for trying all of the various text or possible passwords within the file. This is a significant advantage to the examiner when the dictionary file is created from a listing of all words on the hard disk, a feature available within FTK.

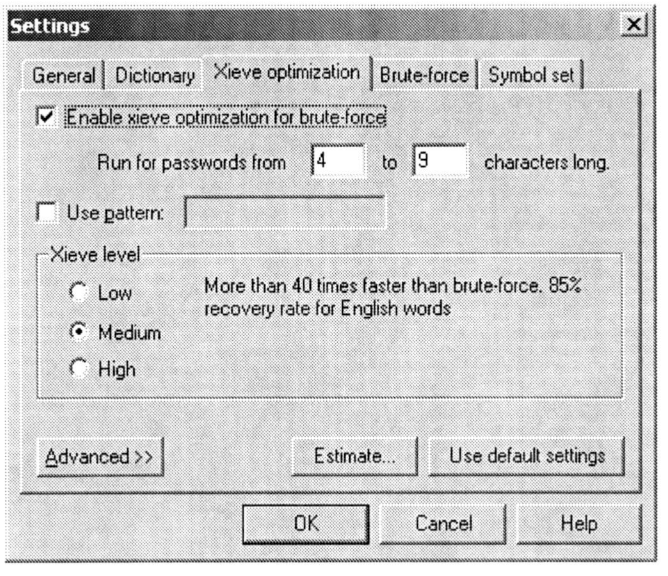

Figure 114

The brute force option permits the use of all possible combinations of characters and is most likely to recover small but weak passwords in a relatively short period of time.

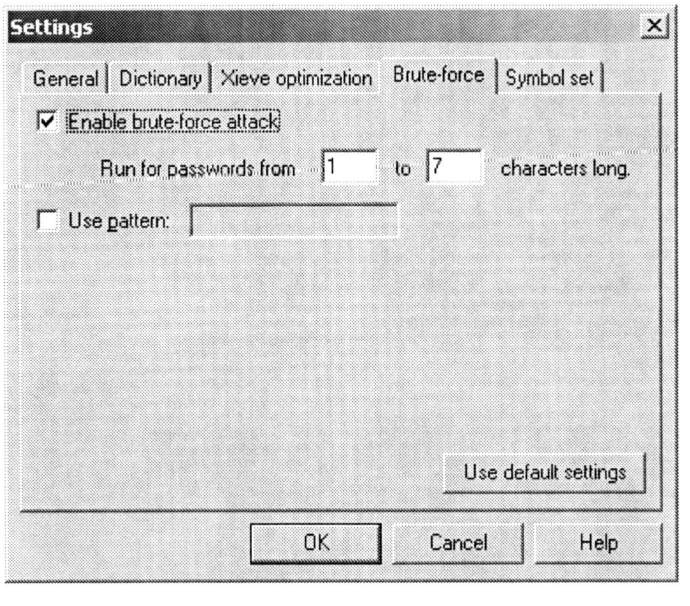

Figure 115

The options that are available for a brute force attack are beneficial in that if the auditor or examiner has an idea of the length of the password, time will not be wasted using options outside of the targeted parameters. For example, if the password to be recovered is under a domain control of the network or operating system, and the password policy prevents less than six character passwords, the examiner can initiate the recovery process beginning at six characters.

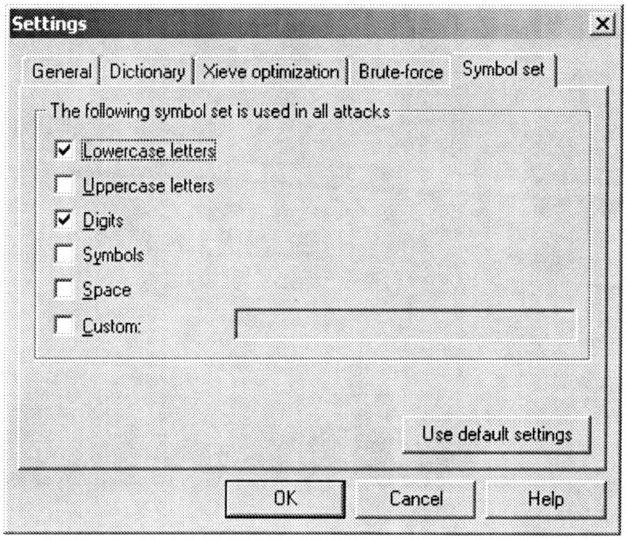

Figure 116

To import a dictionary file, select the File, Restore option.

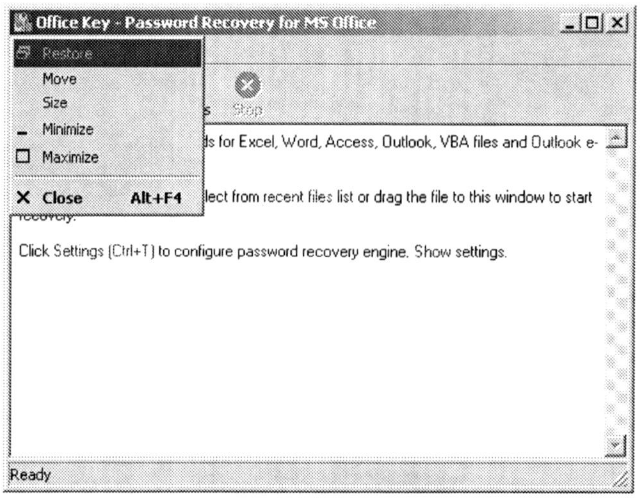

Figure 117

Known Plaintext Attack

The possibility of a password recovery is significantly more if the examiner has access to the hard drive the user used to create the encrypted file. As a result of autosave features and other user activities, the possibility of pieces of that file or that files password being discovered are greater and may be used as a reference in the current recovery attempts. Once such advantage is that of a known plain text attack.

A known plaintext attack involves the recovery of password protected ZIP files and will work only if the exact same version of software used to ZIP and password protect the file is used to recover. Thus, if you have access to the drive used to create the encrypted ZIP file, you may have a copy of one of the files within the encrypted ZIP file. To be successful in this process the examiner should collect as many ZIP file programs and versions as possible.

For example, an examiner locates a password protected ZIP file and identifies several files within. The examiner would then search the rest of the drive image for any files with the same name of one of the files within the encrypted ZIP file. If a copy of one of the files is located, it can be used to recover the remaining files within the ZIP image.

Send the identified or suspected plaintext file to a ZIP file using the same version of ZIP software used in the ZIP file to be recovered. Sometimes the examiner may need to attempt several different versions to make sure the correct one has been used. The next step to initiate this form of recovery is to initialize the Passware program and select the ZIP Key recovery option.

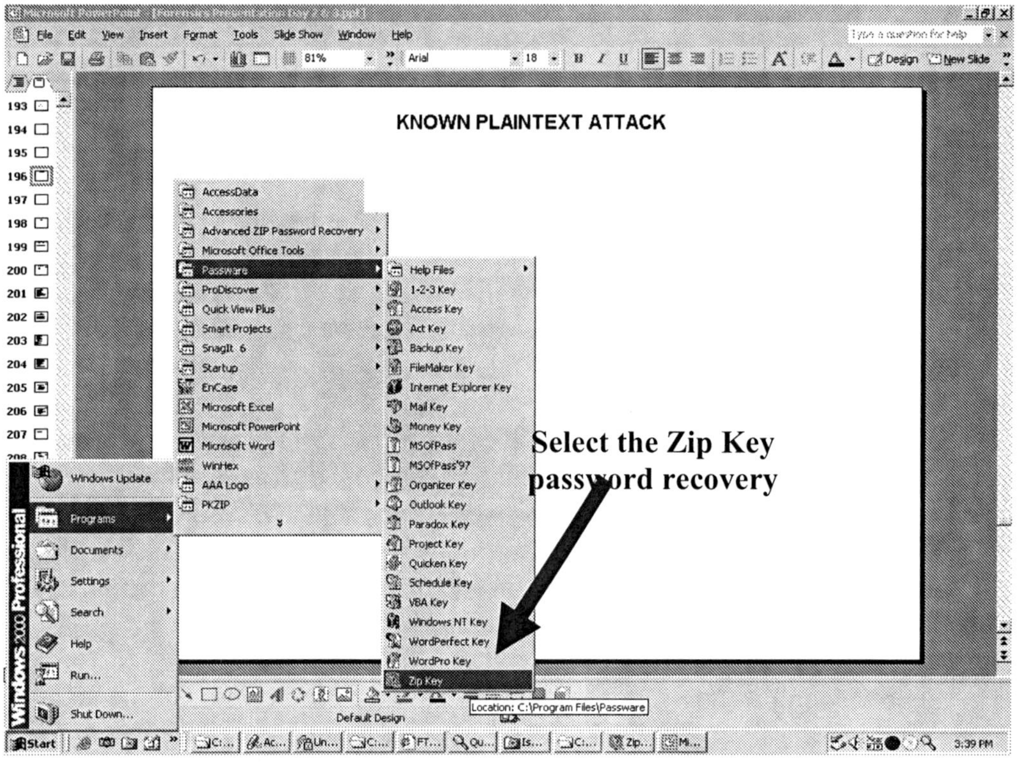

Figure 118

Then select the Settings option.

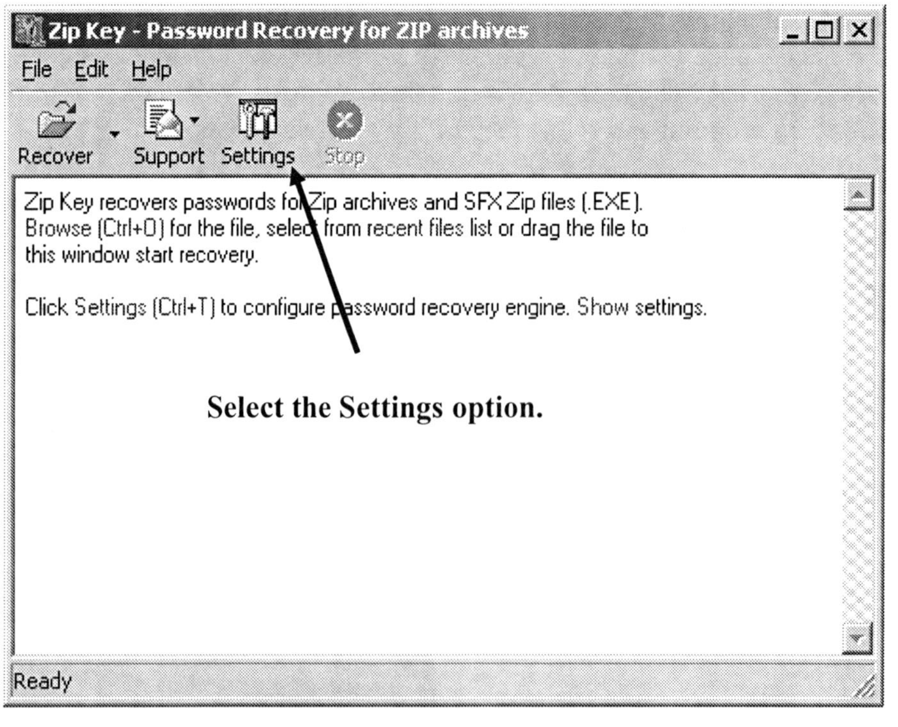

Figure 119

This will provide the following window. At this point select the Known Plaintext option.

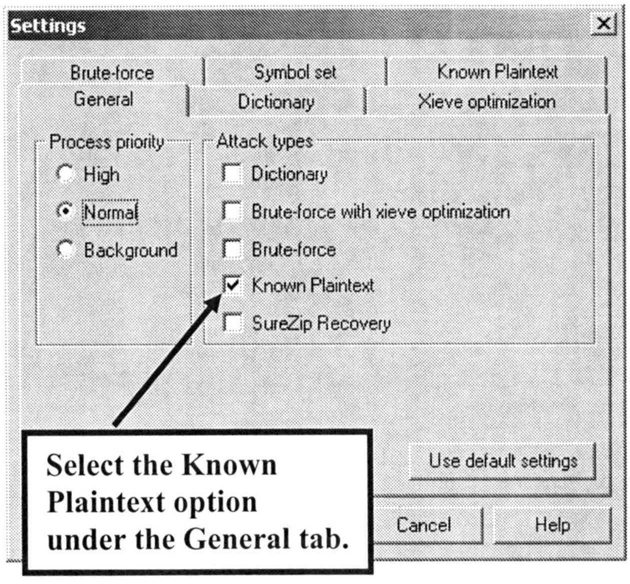

Figure 120

Next, select the Enable Known Plaintext attack button and navigate the Known Plaintext file browser window to the selected ZIP file that contains the plaintext version of the encrypted file within the ZIP file.

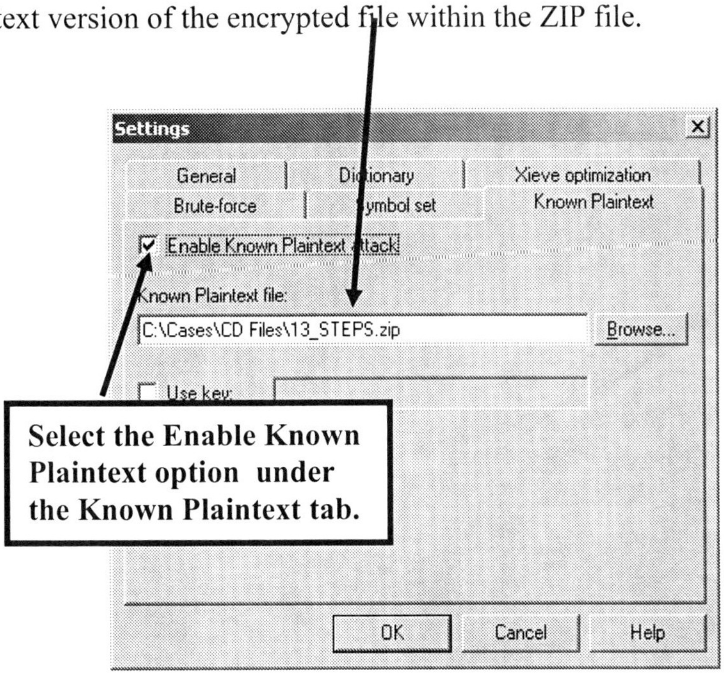

Figure 121

Once these settings have been selected you are ready to attempt the recovery.

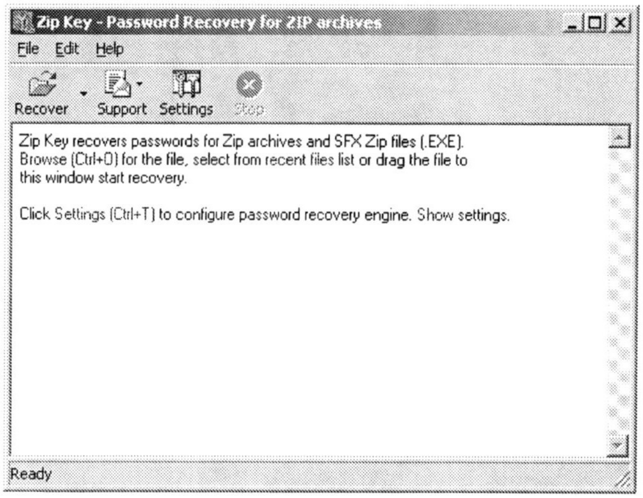

Figure 122

Drag and drop the ZIP file to be recovered into the ZIP Key recovery window. This will begin the process.

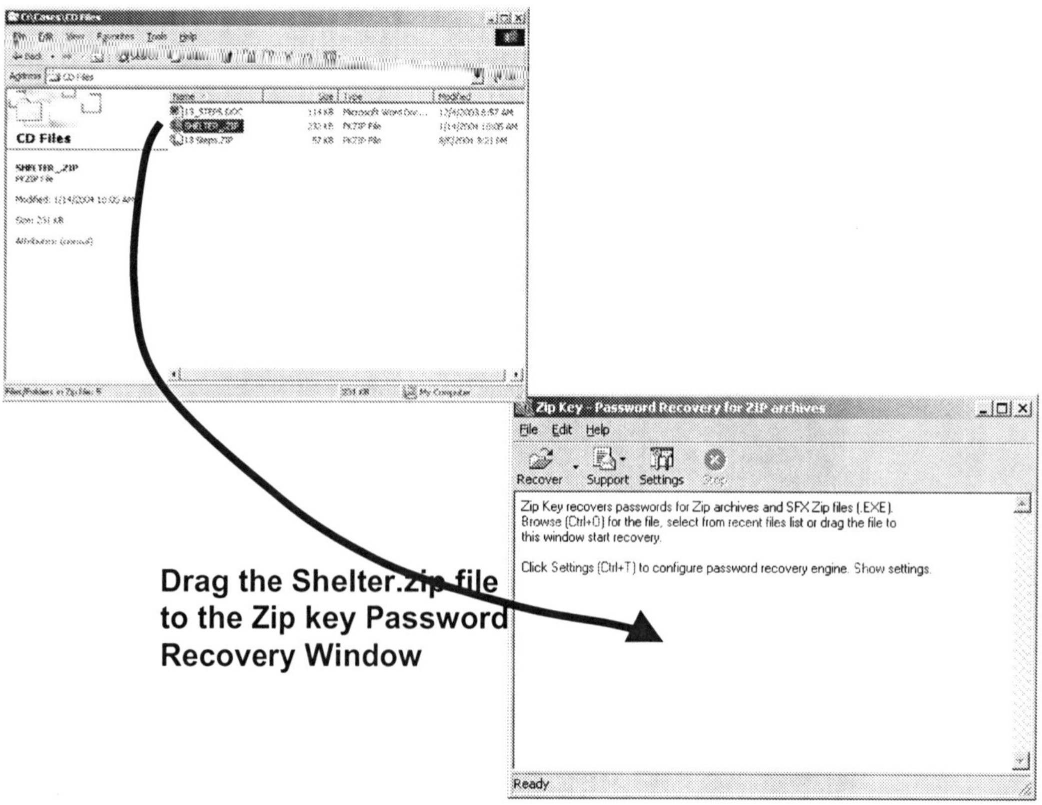

Figure 123

The password recovery process will begin.

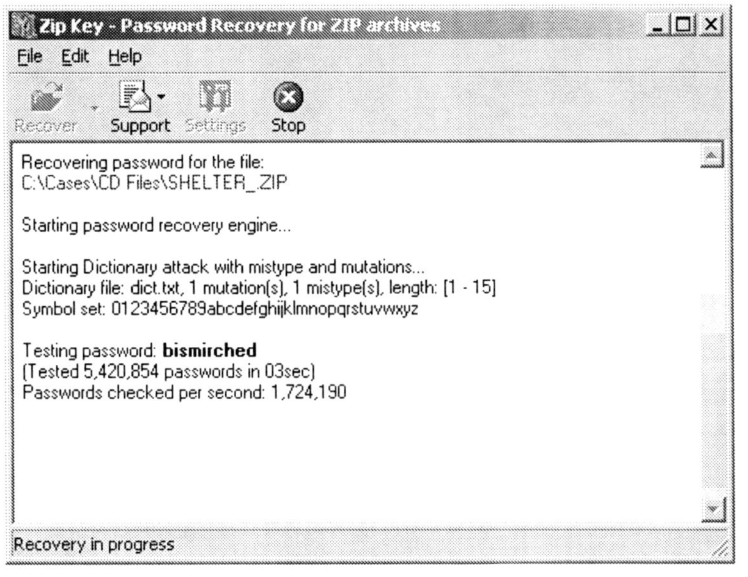

Figure 124

If the recovery is successful, the password will be provided within the recovery window.

Perform Forensics Lab # 14

TITLE: Microsoft Word Password Recovery Using Passware

OBJECTIVE:

To recover a Microsoft password protected Word file using Passware.

Perform Forensics Lab # 15

TITLE: Microsoft Excel Password Recovery Using Passware

OBJECTIVE:

To recover a Microsoft password protected Excel file using Passware.

Perform Forensics Lab # 16

TITLE: Forensics Known Plaintext ZIP File Password Recovery

OBJECTIVE:

To perform a known plaintext attack password recovery of a ZIP file using Passware.

Perform Forensics Lab # 17

TITLE: Forensics Known Plaintext ZIP File Password Recovery

what?

OBJECTIVE:

To perform a known plaintext attack password recovery of a ZIP file using Passware.

Perform Forensics Lab # 18

TITLE: Password Policy Search Lab

OBJECTIVE:

To increase awareness of password policies and why they mandate lengths and password age.

The Operating Systems Role

Every single bit, byte, nibble, sector, cluster, sector address, track, format, file table or data file on the media is written by hardware under the control of software.

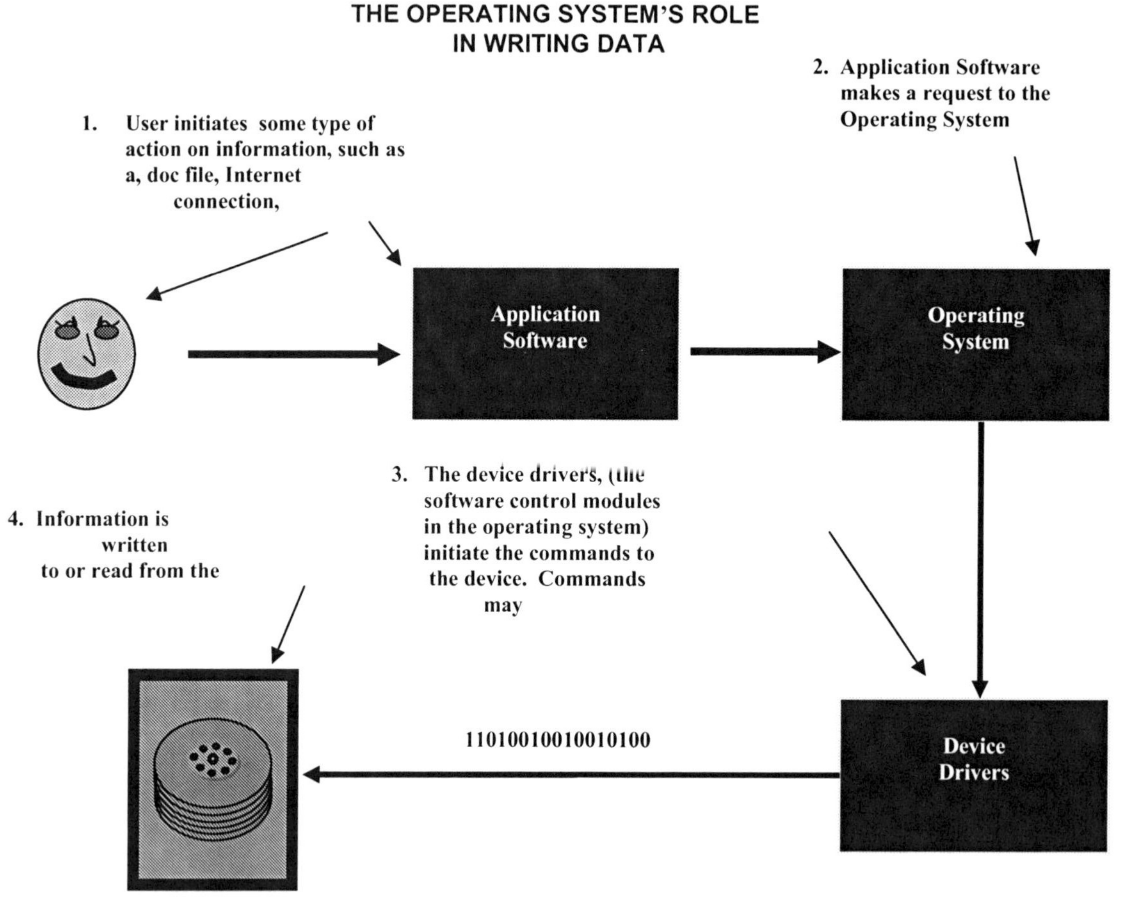

Figure 125

ALL MEDIA MUST HAVE SOFTWARE TO COMMUNICATE TO IT

Hardware that performs variable activities requires instructions. These instructions may be housed within a computer chip (BIOS or Firmware), or they may be external to the processor board (operating systems), or a combination of both. All personal computers are designed to take advantage of both. Software for a computer system comes from various locations:

- Operating System Support
- Device Drivers
- Application Software
- Device Firmware

One of the roles of the operating system is to map the surface of the hard disk for the placement, recovery, maintenance and recovery of data and information. But before a hard disk can be used for the placement of user data and information it must be mapped for the operating system to understand. One of these mappings is known as partitioning.

Partitioning is the logical formation of data structures on the disk. To the user it is something as simple as the difference between the C: and D: drives. To the operating system it is a format pattern bounded by a logical isolation from another format pattern.

Drive Partitions

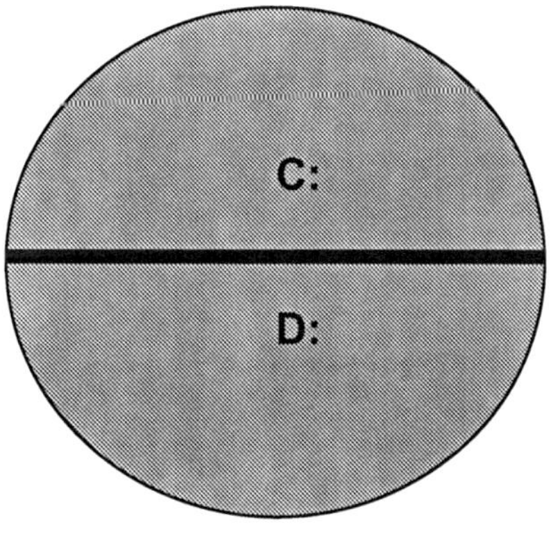

Figure 126

The Physical Drive

The examiner can consider the disk drive as two components, the hardware and the software. The hardware component consists of the physical drive and includes the disk platters, the disk drive motor, the printed circuit board, the interface and power connections, and any other tangible component that can be held in ones hand.

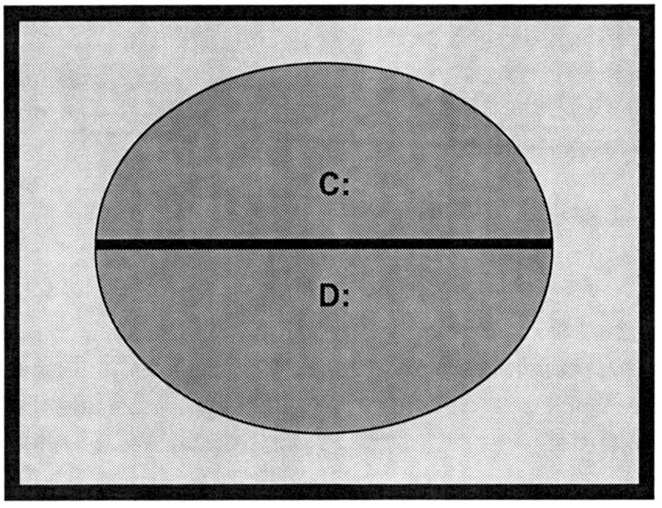

Figure 127

Logical Drives are Software Divisions of the Physical Component

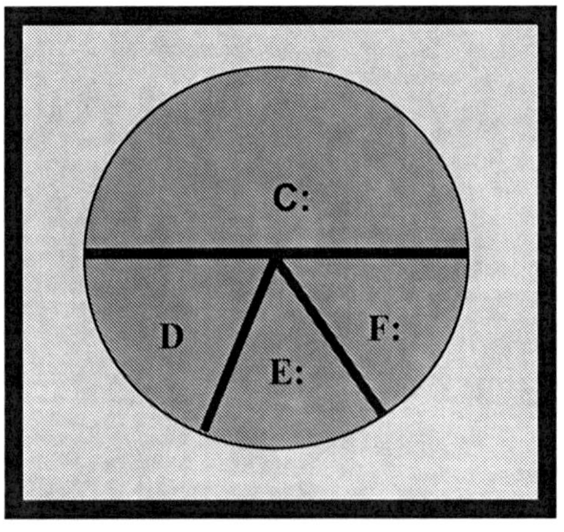

Figure 128

Extended Partition

Hard drive may have only one extended partition, however, this extended partition may have an additional 23 logical partitions. Each logical partition may contain its own operating system, format pattern or file structure. The initial primary partition + a maximum of 23 logical partitions in the extended partition can provide a total of 24 partitions.

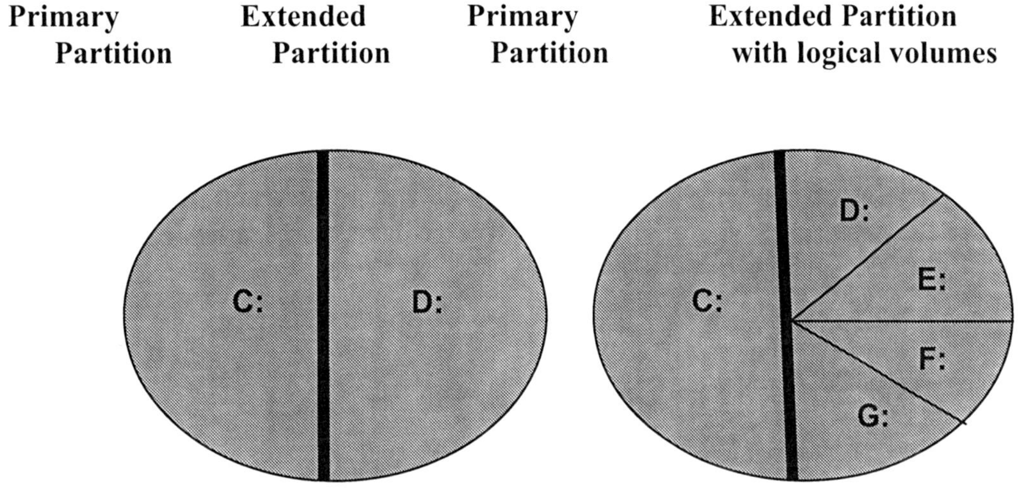

Figure 129

For a hard disk to contain a Windows operating system it must go through several steps of preparation. The first step is to identify the logical size of the drive. By logical, this means, if the physical drive capacity is 200 GB, the drive may be prepared to use the entire 200 GB for one partition or it may be "sliced" into smaller components known as partitions. For example, the owner / user of a 200 GB hard drive may desire to have the primary partition consist of 100 GB of disk space and use the remaining 100 GB for either another operating system or as a database for specific types of files.

Once the size of the primary partition has been determined, the FDISK command can be used to adjust the size of the partition. To do this the user boots off of another media such as a floppy, CD-ROM or other device. They then execute the RUN command to get a command prompt. Once the command prompt is present the user enters the FDISK command. Although outside the scope of this training program, the learner should become familiar with the FDISK command and the concept of partitioning.

Once the primary partition has been created, the size of the extended partition may be determined as well. Generally it is the remaining space of the drive, in this case 100 GB, although using all of the remaining space is not required. After the primary partition has been defined using the FDISK program, the partition must be formatted. This is done using the format command.

As an analogy for these operations, consider the construction of an office building. The building walls define the entire size of the building. This is the partition. The layout and construction of the individual offices may represent the format. This is the typical construction of a logical format.

How this is significant to the forensic examiner is that there are many places to hide or lose data within this building. Not all of the building is used by all of the inhabitants all of the time. Additionally, each office area may have specific amounts of information in it. The amount of information and how it is stored and in which office is a function of the operating system. Thus, we introduce the concept of RAM slack.

RAM Slack

RAM slack is created as a result of memory (RAM) data being used to fill the memory buffers prior to a hard disk write. This is because of the requirements that the operating system write data in even block sizes. This is to accommodate a consistent and efficient maintenance and management of the files on the disk. Random sizes would result in immediate fragmentation and have serious adverse effects on the performance of the system.

RAM slack may contain "anything" in RAM at that time. In actuality it is remnants of previous operations in RAM. It may consist of a left over e-mail, part of a graphic image or some other text file. Again, it is produced as a result of the operating system writing data to the disk drive in consistent block sizes. RAM slack pertains to only the last sector of a file. An estimated 25% of hard disk drive space is File Slack

File Slack on Media

In addition to RAM slack, file slack is an area of interest to the forensic examiner. For example, consider the following examples of track space on a disk. Initially, the space is blank with the exception of format information.

BLANK

Track 0

BLANK

Track 1

BLANK

Track 2

Figure 130

File information is written to the disk and allocated to the various clusters by the operating system. Each file has its own defined space on the disk.

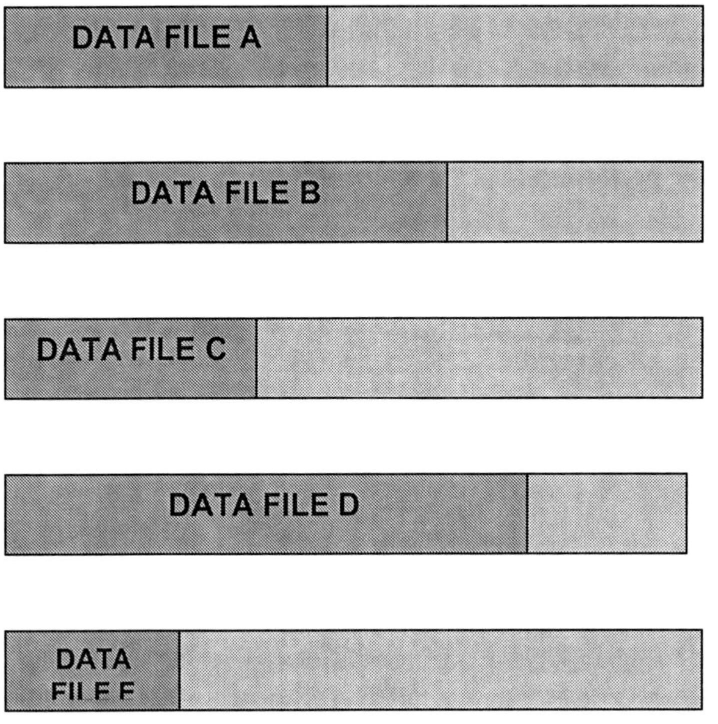

Figure 131

Now consider that these files are deleted by the user and their addresses become available to the operating system for future allocation of files. Remember, when a file is deleted, it is not erased or overwritten, its address is made available.

Overwriting Files

Now consider that the first file, File A is overwritten by File F. The Green portion represents File A while the red outline represents the new file, File F. Now consider File B is overwritten by File G. File C has been overwritten by File H, etc.

By observing the following in Figure 132 you can see how new files overwrite deleted file space. This example shows that remnants of File A may exist immediately following the new File F, and remnants of File C may exist immediately after File C.

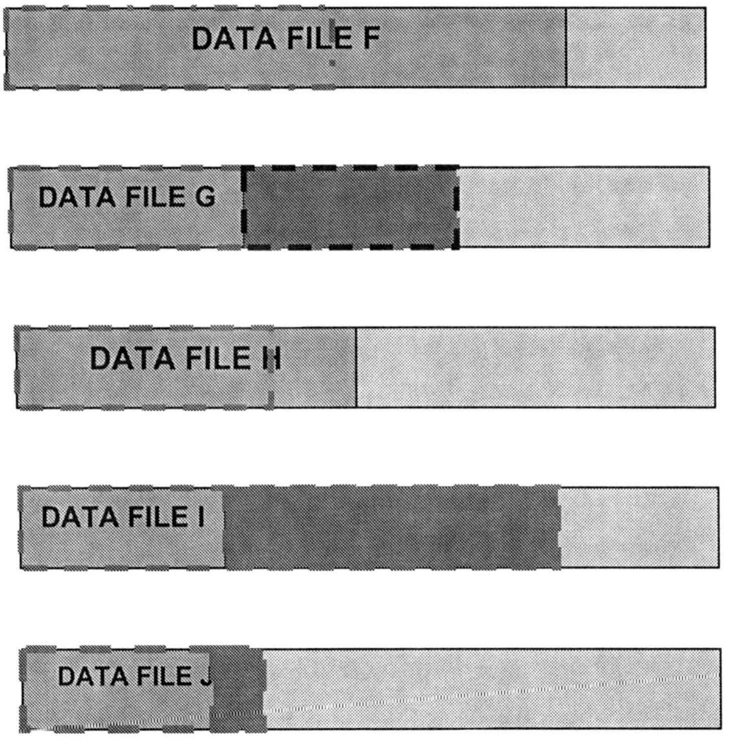

Figure 132

The file sizes may vary however the block sizes do not and are consistent by the particular operating system parameters. For example, the actual logical file size of a particular file may be 2 K in size, however, the physical file size may be 8 K, the size of the cluster. A 9 or 10 K file size would result in a 16 K physical file size due to the file requiring two clusters to be written.

These areas are known as file slack and may be recovered by various acquisition and analysis tools and techniques. One such technique is known as Data Carving, an option available in FTK.

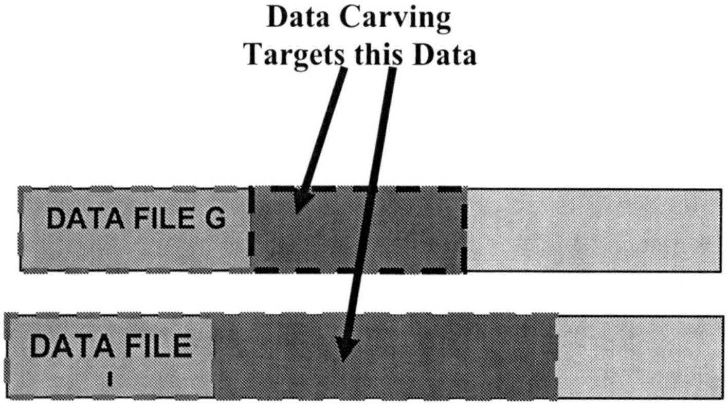

Figure 133

File slack may be processed by multiple tools, including;

- Diskedit
- WinHex
- Encase
- FTK
- NTI Software Tools
    - Getslack
    - Getfree
    - Seejunk

To process file slack the examiner must have a forensically sound image of the media.

SWAP Files

Another potential gold mine of information may be found in the swap file. A swap file is that file on the hard disk that is used as a virtual memory. The operating systems VMM software "swaps" data between the hard disk and a reserved area in RAM (Main memory)

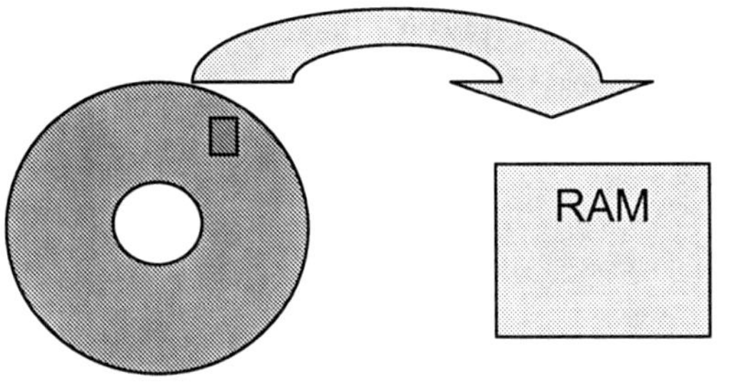

Figure 134

Swap files may vary in size and may be adjusted by the user or according to settings of the operating system. Swap file are actual files and have specific names. Pagefile.sys for NT file systems and Swapfile.sys for Windows 9x operating systems. Some default file sizes are:

Default size in NT4 = size of physical memory + 12 MB

Default size in W2K = size of physical memory times 1.5

Swap files typically contain binary data but may also contain human readable information. Additionally, under Windows 2003 and below operating systems the swap file can not be encrypted.

Formatting the Hard Drive

Formatting is the process of laying down the track addressing data so that it can be assigned information or files at a later date. Without the drive being formatted, it would not be possible to place data in an identifiable and logical manner. As an analogy, a format may be compared to a city. The city has streets and addresses. The city phone book (MFT or FAT) contains the address information for each house (cluster) and the contents of each cluster. Thus, a format maps the surface of the media into tracks and sectors. There are two types of formats, a low level format and a high level format.

Low level format –

This is generally performed in the factory during the drives performance validation test. The purpose of a low level format is to prepare the media for a high level format created by each individual operating system. It accomplishes this by placing a format template, or servo pattern on the disk that permits the read / write head to follow in order to place logical format information (high level format) on it.

A high level format is where the addresses information is written to the hard disk by following the low level servo pattern placed there previously. Thus, the sector, cluster and track numbers are written and recorded in either the FAT or the MFT. And as stated previously, a cluster consists of two or more sectors and information recorded on the drive is recorded by cluster number.

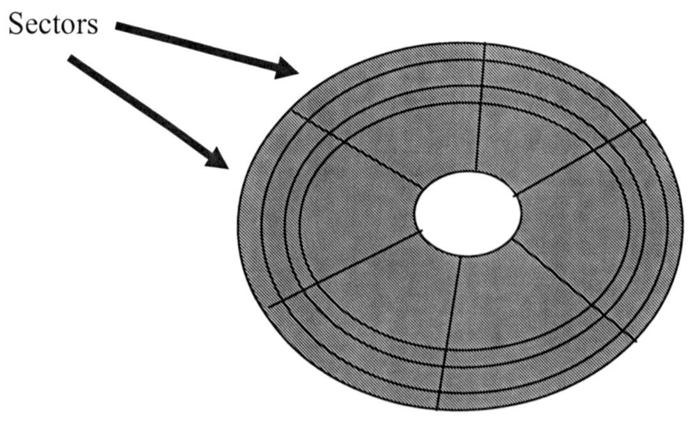

Figure 135

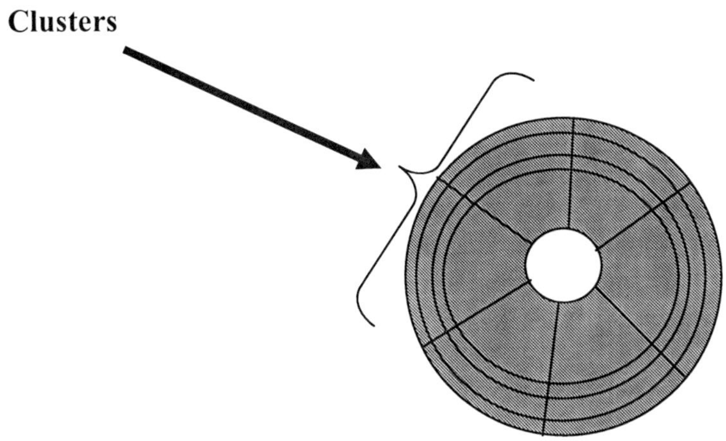

Figure 136

Logical Structure of a Sector

Figure 137

A sector is generally 512 bytes in size. A 1 K cluster will consist of two sectors. (512 x 2 = 1024 bytes = 1 K). A 2 K cluster will consist of four sectors (512 x 4 = 2048 bytes = 4 K).

Erasing Files and Unallocated Space

As previously stated, deleting files does not erase them. Deleting files only makes that sector and cluster address available to the operating system for a future write operation. And random or variable deletion of files on the disk results in fragmentation of the logical sequencing of the information. Thus, deleted files on a disk:

1. Become recoverable with a computer forensic analysis of the hard drive.

2. Stay on the drive until overwritten.

Thus, to remove files from a disk they must be overwritten. There are some drive utility programs that are designed to erase files and remnants of files. These types of programs or applications are commonly referred to as cyber scrubbing programs. Some popular cyber scrubbing programs are Eraser 5.8 and Evidence Eliminator.

As stated previously, some cyber scrubbing programs are designed to scrub the disk if the system is shut down without a preconfigured authorization. Evidence Eliminator is one such program. This is one more reason that the forensic examiner must pull the plug and not shut down a target or evidence system.

THERE ARE TWO FAT TABLES ON EACH BOOTABLE DEVICE

The FAT or MFT may be compared to a phone book. It contains the address of every allocated cluster on the disk. The data area of the FAT begins with the second cluster address and each FAT supports up to 64K cluster sizes. The larger the disk drive, the larger the allocation unit (cluster size). The second FAT is a backup FAT in case the first FAT becomes corrupted. Older disk drive technology that contained less than 32 MB, allocation units were limited to 512 bytes.

PARTITION SIZES

Type of FAT	Min Partition Size	Max Partition Size
FAT12	1.5 KB	510.75 MB
FAT16	2.0435 KB	8190.75 MB
FAT32	Approx 32 MB	32 TB

UNALLOCATED SPACE

Unallocated space is that space on the media where data can be written, i.e. available space. Unallocated space becomes available when either files are deleted or the space was never allocated. Unallocated space that becomes available as a result of a file deletion has left over data in it. This information may be of value to a computer forensic examiner. This may be compared to resetting the all the addresses and phone numbers in a telephone book, without changing the contents of the residences. The contents of each residence (cluster) will be changed as needed, i.e., overwritten when needed.

As may be appreciated, there may be significant amounts of file slack on the media. As disk drives get bigger the methods and time required to examine all of the file slack may be prohibitive. The data carving option of FTK provides a valuable tool for performing such analysis. Data carving involves searching through file slack for particular types of files, including;

. jpeg
. gif
. bitmap
- Hypertext

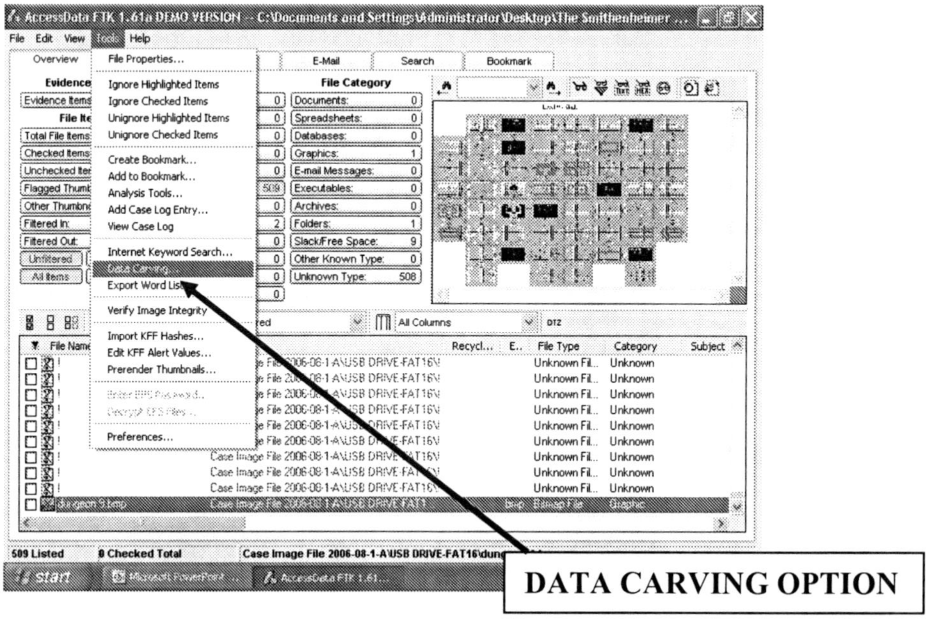

Figure 138

Data carving is an option that can be selected during the initial setup of the case analysis or at a later point during the examination. The advantage of selecting it during the setup is that it may identify such files initially during the analysis. The disadvantage is that it is a very time consuming task and may not be desirable in all cases.

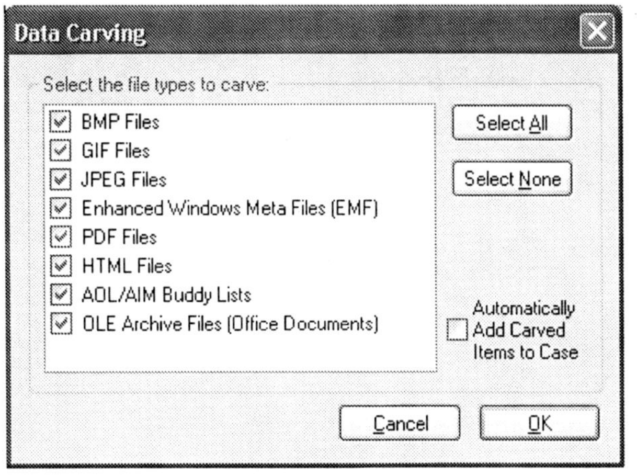

Figure 139

The examiner may select the type of files to be carved from unallocated space. Data carving also will permit the identification of files embedded into other files such as Microsoft Word or Excel Spreadsheet files.

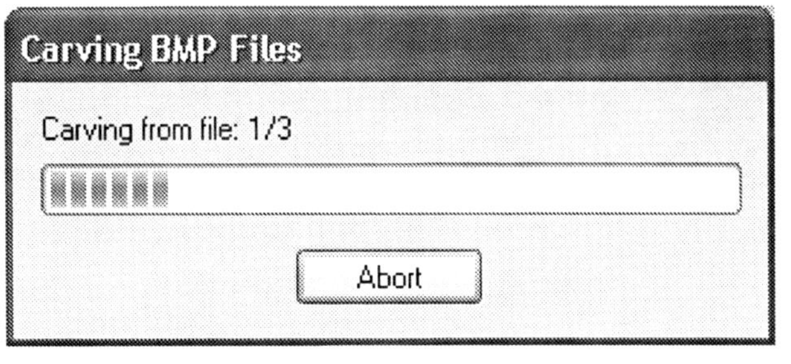

Figure 140

Data carving is a valuable operation and may reclaim;

- Deleted files
- Lost files
- Partially overwritten files

Once identified, these files can then be added to the forensics image file and reviewed for value to the case.

Perform Forensics Lab # 19

TITLE: Data Carving Using Case Image 2005-25

OBJECTIVE:

To retrieve data files, picture files, partial files and other documents from disk free space.

Perform Forensics Lab # 20

TITLE: Analyze Case Image file 2005-30

OBJECTIVE:

To analyze a particular media to determine if any information of evidentiary value is contained within and to report on it.

CD-ROM / DVD Disks

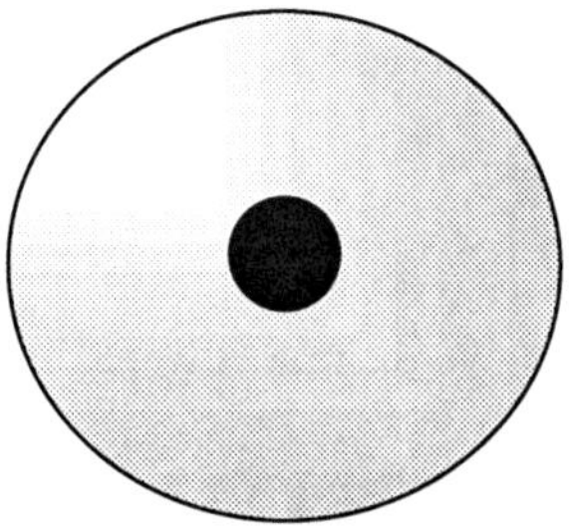

Although CD-ROM and DVD disk technology is not dependent upon magnetic recording, like a hard disk it must have an addressing scheme to place and locate data. CD-ROM formats do not use individual and discrete tracks like hard disk but rely on a spiral pattern originating from the center of the disk where hard disk formats begin their track numbering sequences from the outer most part of the disk. In some cases, if additional data is added to the CD-ROM disk, a new spiral pattern is written, beginning at the end of the original spiral pattern. Each spiral data pattern is referred to as a session.

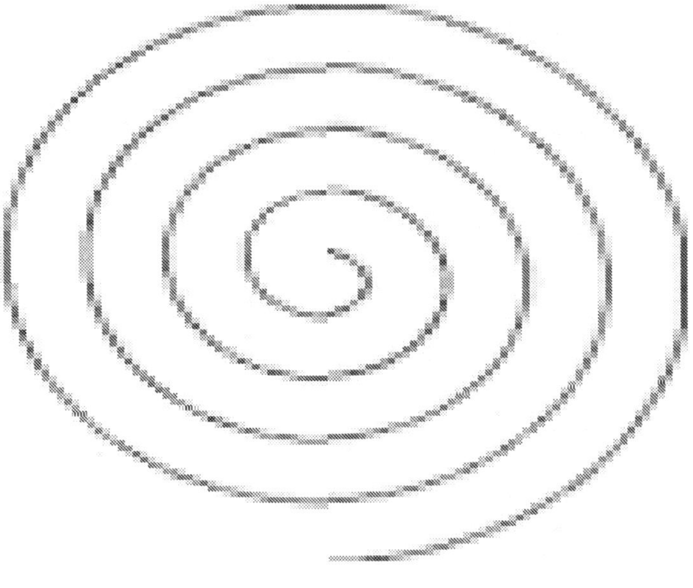

Figure 141

Continuous Spiral Session
Instead of Individual Tracks

How the operating system and various applications interact with CD-ROM formats varies. When a new session is created on a CD-ROM disk, the previous session is sometimes no longer visible or available to the operating system. Thus, a hidden session is created merely by additional writes to some CD-ROM formats. Since the operating system does not present or report these hidden sessions to the users, they are sometimes used to conceal files.

This CD-ROM disk has a hidden session on it, however, it is not displayed by the operating system. Only the last (closed) session is identified.

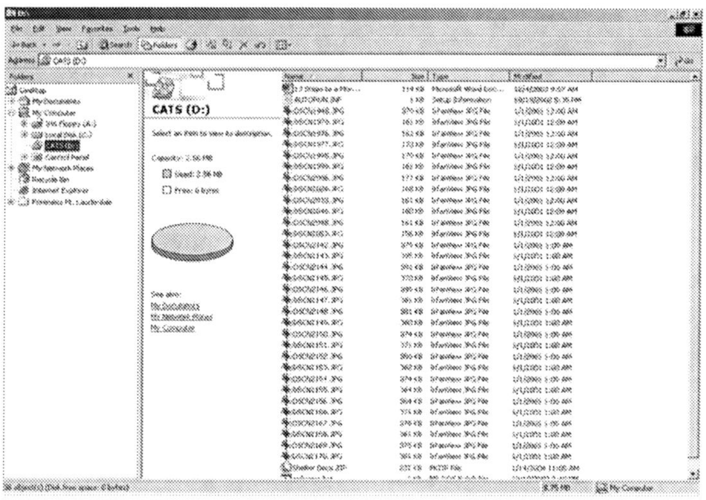

Figure 142

View this same CD-ROM disk with an application that was designed to display all sessions and the hidden files are readily identified. This particular tool is known as ISO Buster.

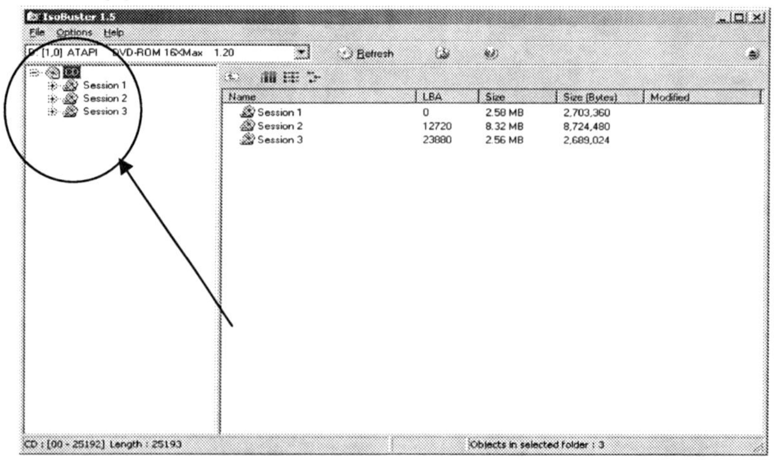

Figure 143

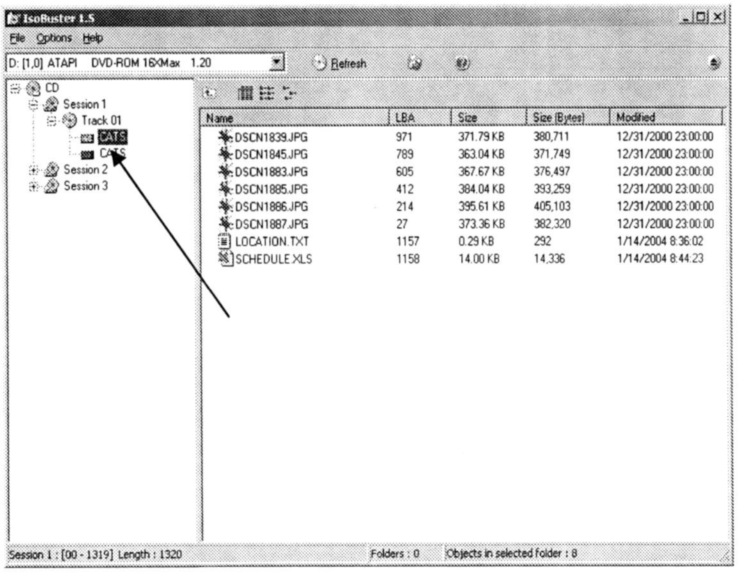

Figure 144

Selecting a previous session will expand its contents.

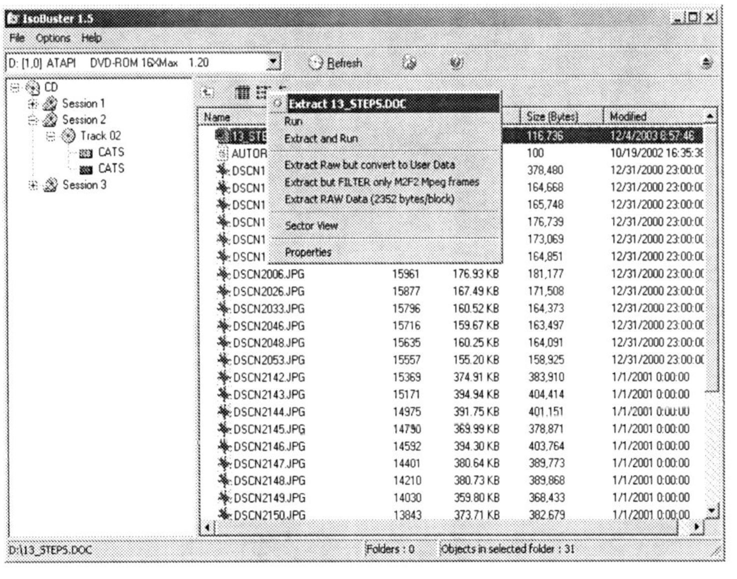

Figure 145

The examiner may then select individual or all files and right click to export each file to a folder for further examination. Figures 145 and 146.

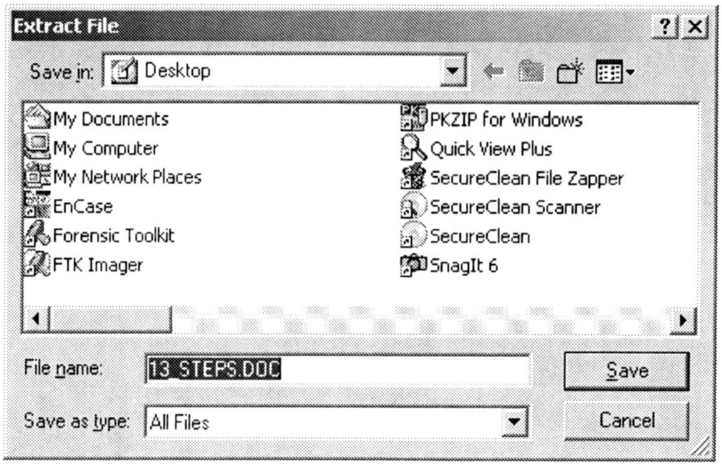
Extract File
Save in: Desktop
My Documents
My Computer
My Network Places
EnCase
Forensic Toolkit
FTK Imager
PKZIP for Windows
Quick View Plus
SecureClean File Zapper
SecureClean Scanner
SecureClean
SnagIt 6
File name:
13_STEPS.DOC
Save
Save as type:
All Files
Cancel

Figure 146

Perform Forensics Lab # 21

TITLE: Using ISO Buster

OBJECTIVE:

To learn how to use ISO Buster for identifying hidden information, or information written with an unknown format on a CD-ROM disk.

Students Use Case 2005 15A CD

Image Captures of Recovered Files

Sometimes it is necessary to demonstrate particular aspects of a recovery, such as various pictures or images, or focus on particular aspects of a picture or image. One such tool that permits easy emphasis for such purposes is an application known as SnagIt. SnagIt permits freehand and entire view screen captures and is useful in capturing;

- Selected parts of images
- Text documents
- Bit maps
- Jpegs
- Other types of files

To install and use SnagIt, click on the SnagIt icon.

Figure 147

The Welcome window will appear.

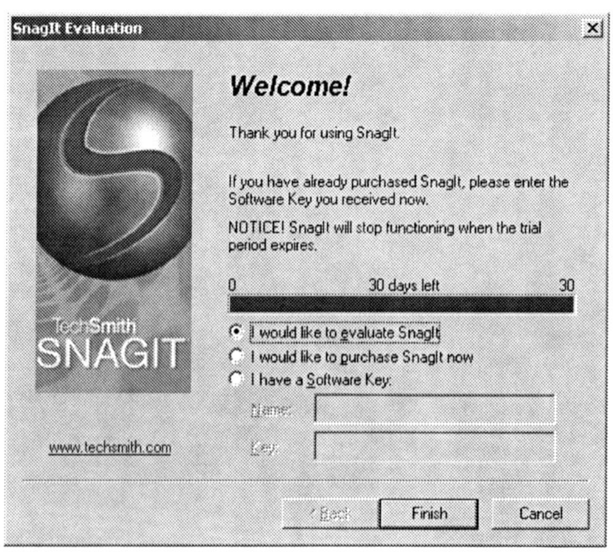

Figure 148

The SnagIT ICON should appear on the desktop.

Figure 149

The SnagIt interface will then appear.

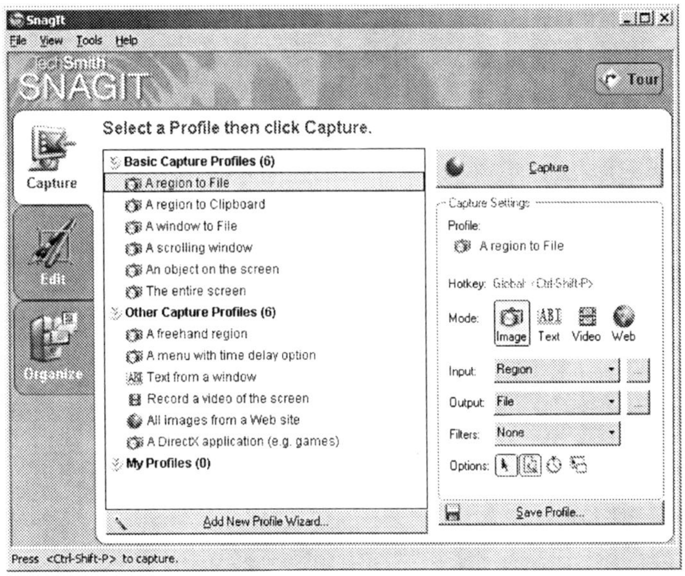

Figure 150

At this point the examiner may open a file and select a portion of it for capture.

Figure 151

Once the examiner has boxed the desired portion of the image, the capture can be saved.

Figure 152

When opened, the captured and saved portion of the image file may appear like this.

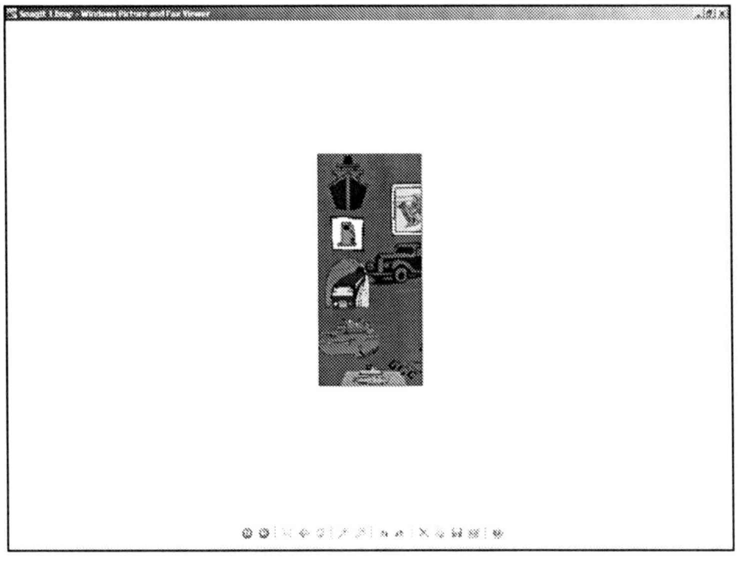

Figure 153

Perform Forensics Lab # 22

TITLE: Using SnagIt

OBJECTIVE:

To learn how to capture screens for use in forensics and other types of reports

Recovery of Non-Standard File Structures on Disk

The computer forensic examiner may encounter a file format that is not native to the Windows operating system or may not have an application to view it. Purchasing applications for each discovered file format may be cost preventative. Thus, a universal tool for revealing non-standard file formats may be used. This particular tool is known as Quick View Plus and will permit viewing of multiple picture and file formats.

Non-standard formats may be viewed with hex editors, however, the presentation is generally limited to only hex and text views. A non-standard file viewed with a hex editor may display the file header and structure of the file, but it does not display embedded picture or image components. One such image program for viewing non-standard file structures is Quick View Plus. Quick View Plus supports over 200 formats

To initialize, click on the Quick View Plus link.

Figure 154

The Quick View Plus application window will appear. Then select the File pull down window.

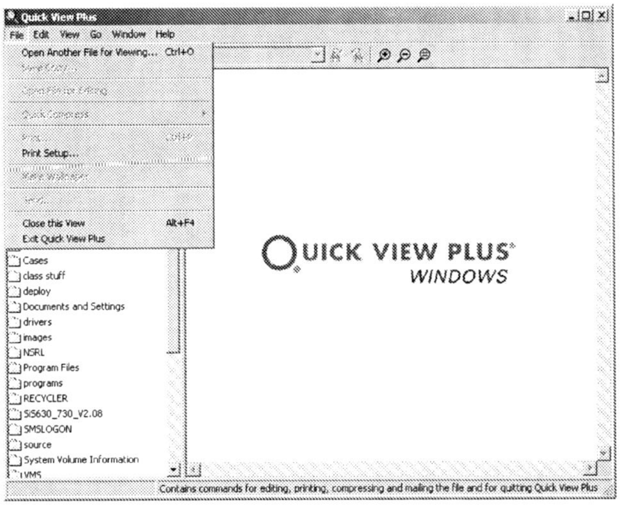

Figure 155

The Select a file to view window will appear.

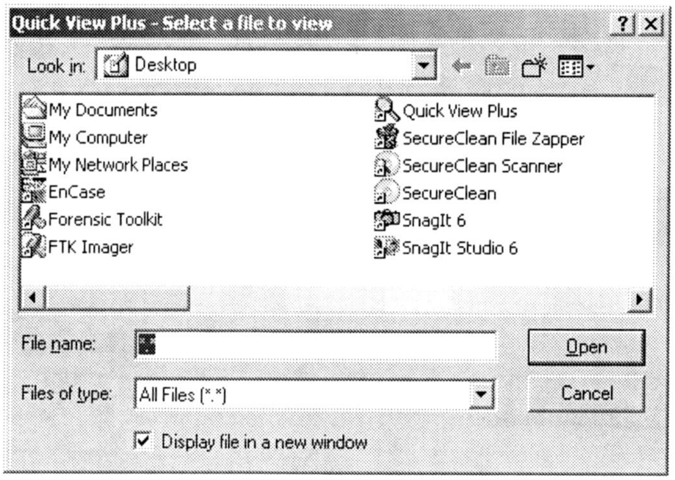

Figure 156

At this point navigate to a .pdf type of file such as the Secret Service Best Practices Guide. This guide can be downloaded from the web and should be read by every computer forensics examiner.

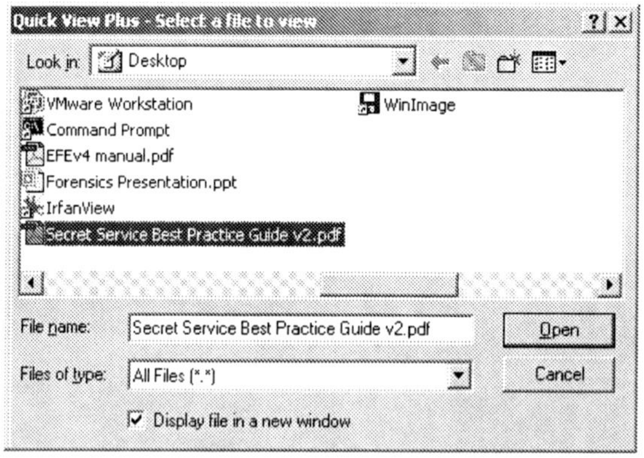

Figure 157

At this point the .pdf file will appear in the view window. This is one demonstration of viewing a file format without the native application.

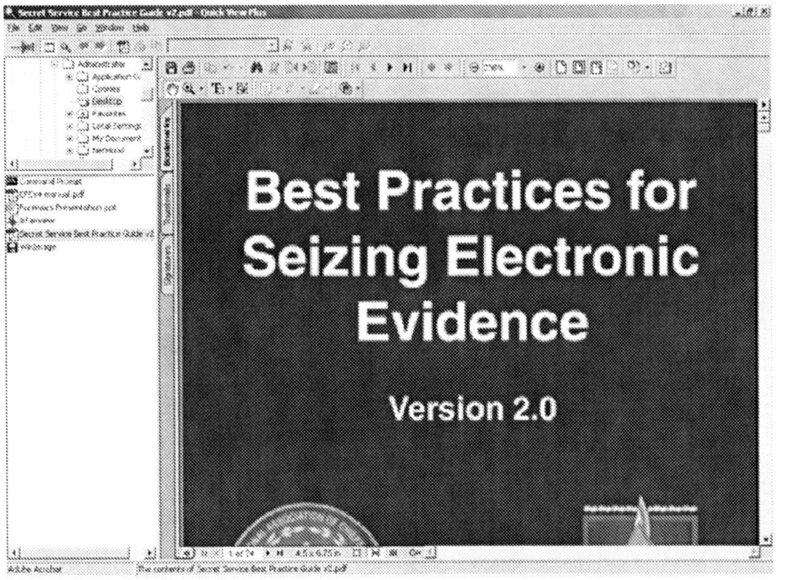

Figure 158

Try this is several different file formats.

Perform Forensics Lab # 23

TITLE: View multiple formats using a single tool.

OBJECTIVE:

Computer forensic examiners encounter multiple file types on a single storage device. Maintaining application software for every file extension type may not be economical for most budgets. The software application Quick View Plus is a single tool that can read more than 200 different formats.

Creating a Word List from an Evidence Drive

As described previously, each word or individual bit string on a target media or image file can be organized into a word list. This word list may be used as a dictionary file for attempted password recoveries. The possibility that a particular password is somewhere on the media, either in file slack or some other text file, is a probability that must be explored when attempting to recover a password from an exported file.

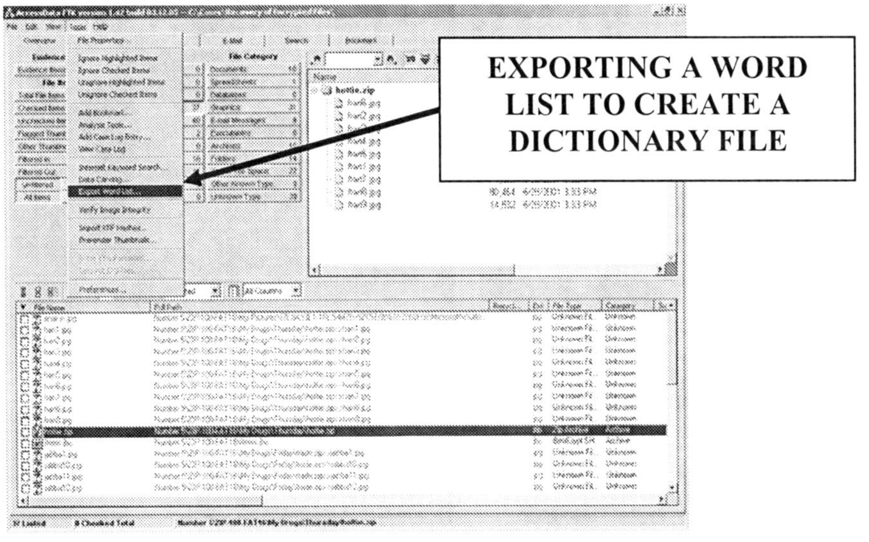

Figure 159

To create the word list, select Tools, then Export Word List. This will index every bit stream, character and word on the drive into an alphabetically organized text file.

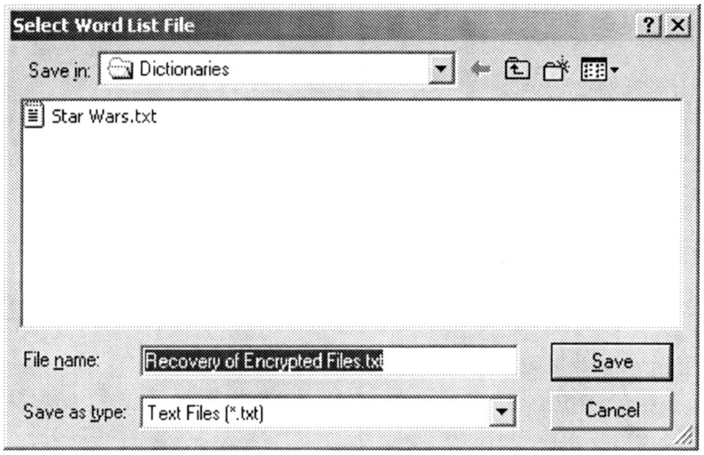

Figure 160

Then select where the word list is to be stored. The examiner should adhere to a naming structure that readily identifies which word file was created from which image. This newly created dictionary file can now be used against the files from the very disk it was recovered from.

Perform Forensics Lab # 24

TITLE: Analyze Case Image file 2005-35

OBJECTIVE:

To analyze a particular media to determine if any information of evidentiary value is contained within and to report on it.

Hashing and Legal Imperatives

One common and highly effective method for ensuring the accuracy of processed data is to establish a hash value for that file or information. Hash values are necessary to demonstrate accuracy, correlation between source and acquired image, and provides a level of confidence to all parties. Hashing of files is a common technique to verify that the file has not been altered, such as the home page of a web site. A hash value is created for the particular web page and its value is stored. Periodically the home page is recalculated and compared with the original. If any data within the file has been lost or changed, a mismatch signals an error and the administrator is notified. This technique is used to validate the integrity of database files as well.

Hashing does not typically include the file name within the hash value calculation. For example, if two files with different names but exact same contents are hashed, the same hash value will result. Figure 161 demonstrates a 128 bit hash value of a file using the MD5 hashing algorithm. Even one character or bit change within that file will result in a totally different hash value for that file.

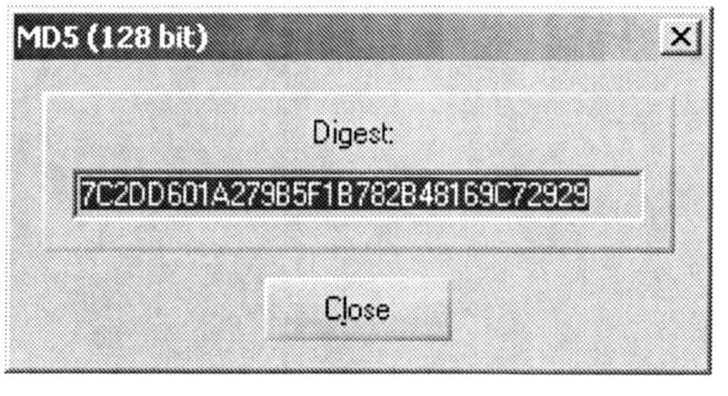

Figure 161

To demonstrate this concept, we will compare the Hash of a specific file for with other hashing applications. Initialize WinHex by clicking on the WinHex shortcut link.

Figure 162

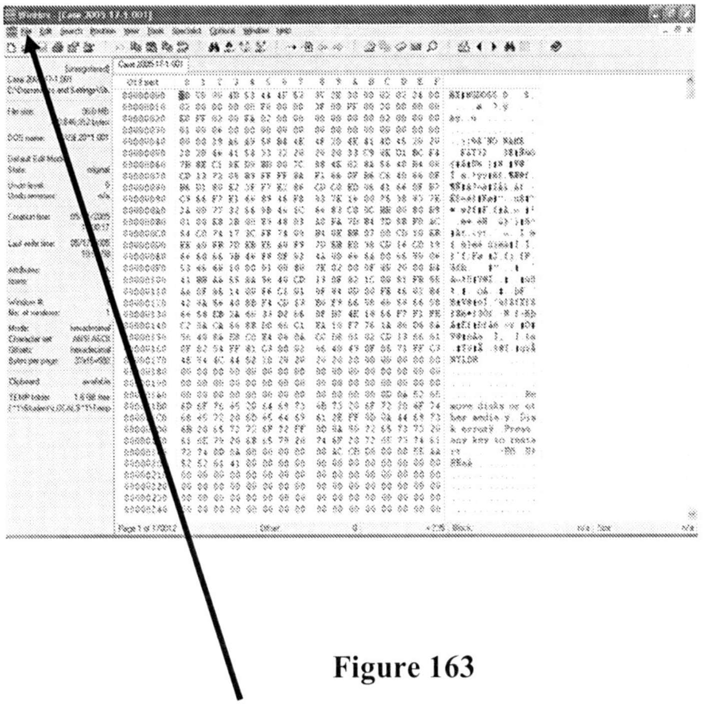

Figure 163

Select File, then Open, then navigate to the desired forensic image file.

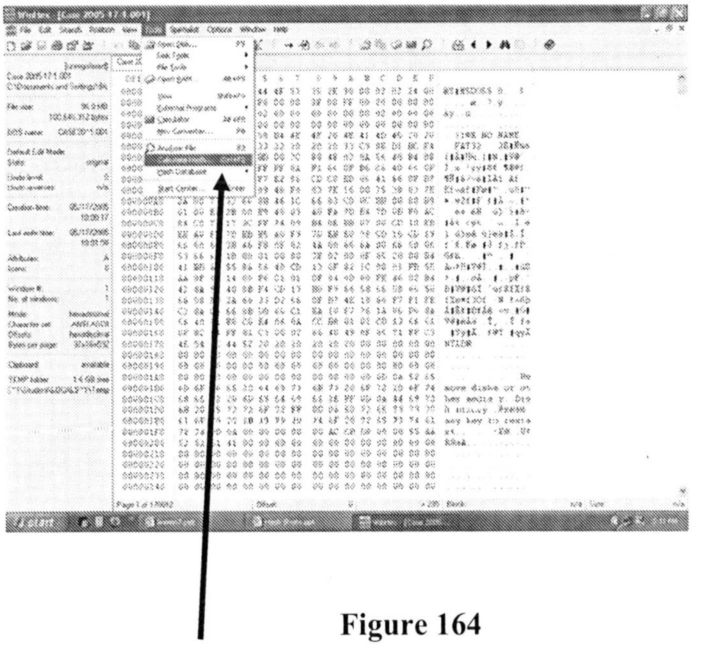

Figure 164

Then select Tools, Calculate Hash.

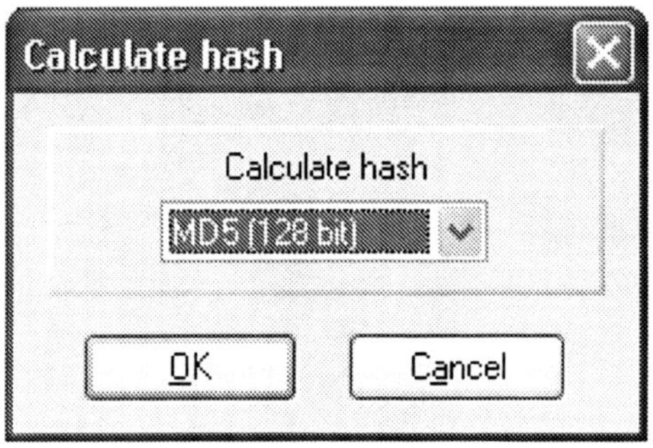

Figure 165

The Calculate hash window will appear. Select MD5 (128 bit).

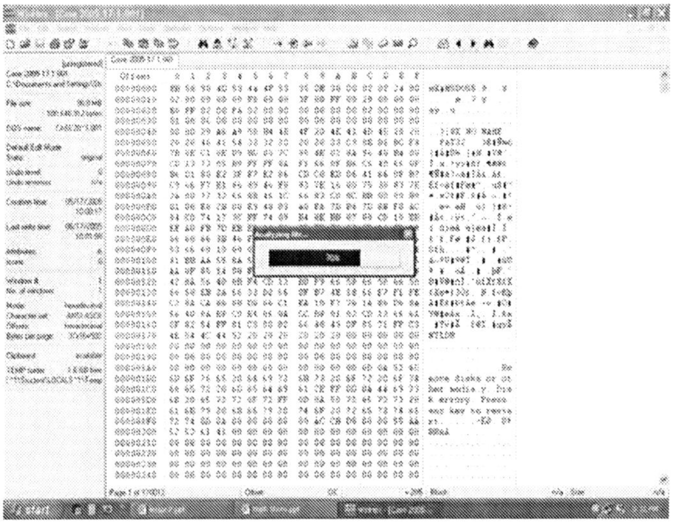

Figure 166

The hashing process will begin and the Analyzing file window will appear. When the hashing algorithm has been processed on this specific file, the hash value will be presented as shown in Figure 167. Record this value.

Figure 167

To demonstrate correlation, download the MD5Extractor program from www.fastream.com/md5extractor.htm and initialize the application.

Figure 168

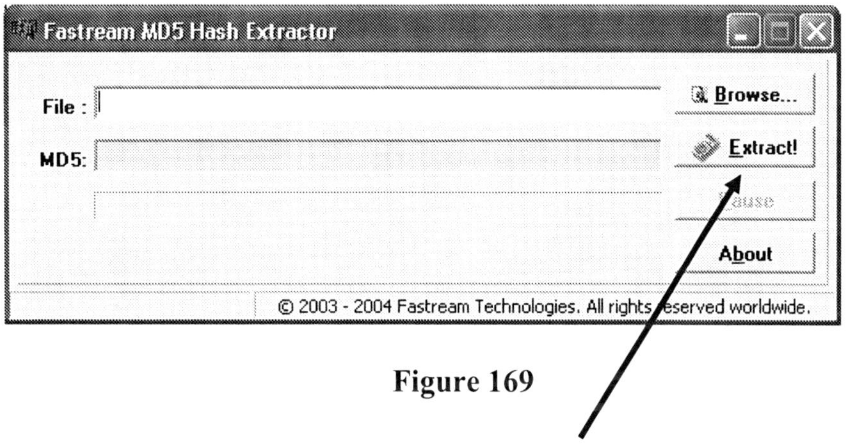

Figure 169

Once the program has initialized, click Browse and navigate to the same acquired forensic image file. Select this file for analysis. (Figure 170)

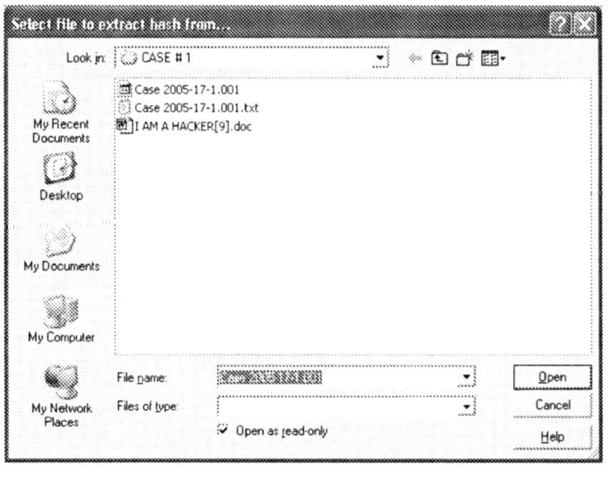

Figure 170

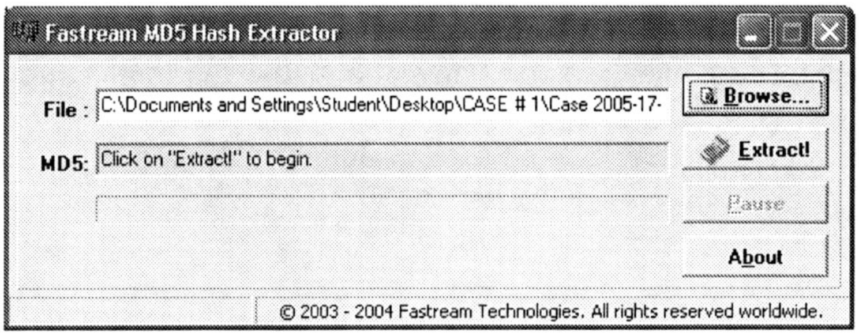

Figure 171

Click Extract. The hash value for the selected image file will begin to be calculated. (Figure 172)

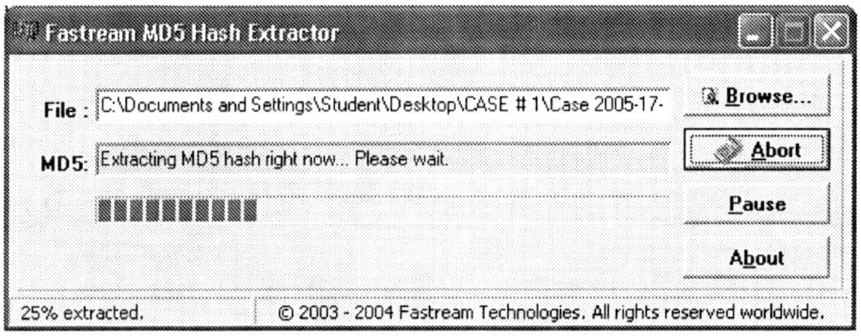

Figure 172

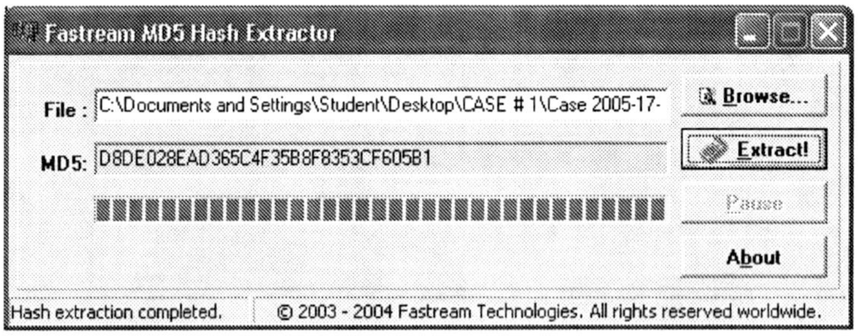

Figure 173

Once completed, the MD5 hash value will be displayed. Record this value.

Another application to demonstrate correlation with hash values is the Accuhash program. Download Accuhash hashing program from the web site http://products.datamation.com/security/perutil/1086981134.html

Once downloaded, click on the link.

Figure 174

The following window should appear. (Figure 175)

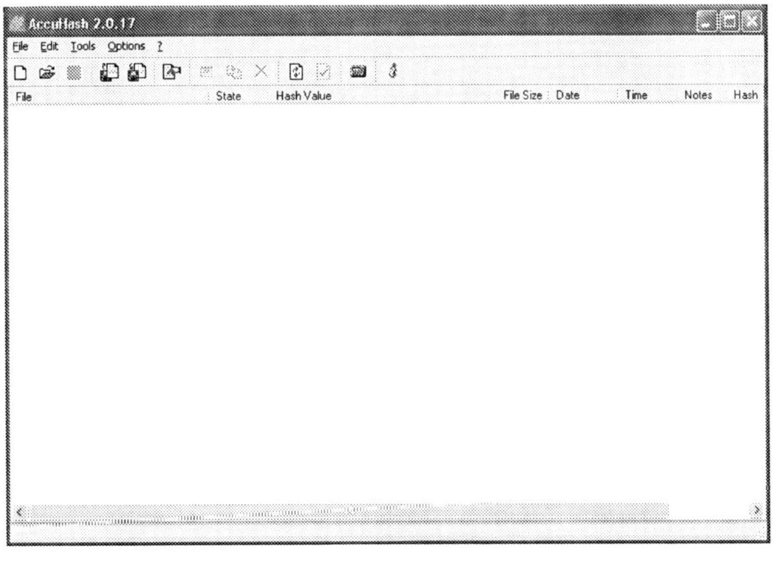

Figure 175

Once the Accuhash program has been initialized, select File, Open, and then navigate to the same forensic image file as used in the previous two examples. Load this file into the application.

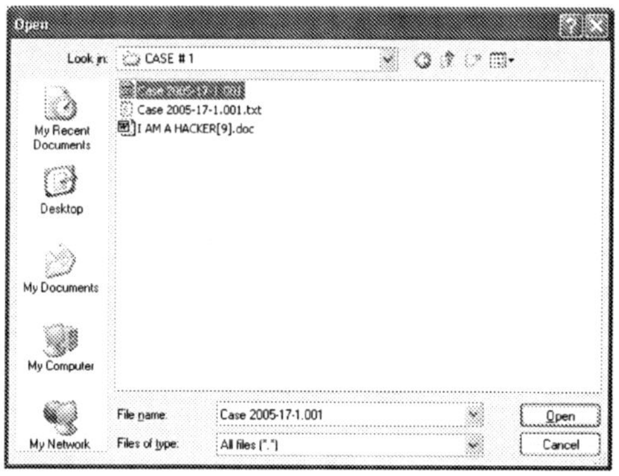

Figure 176

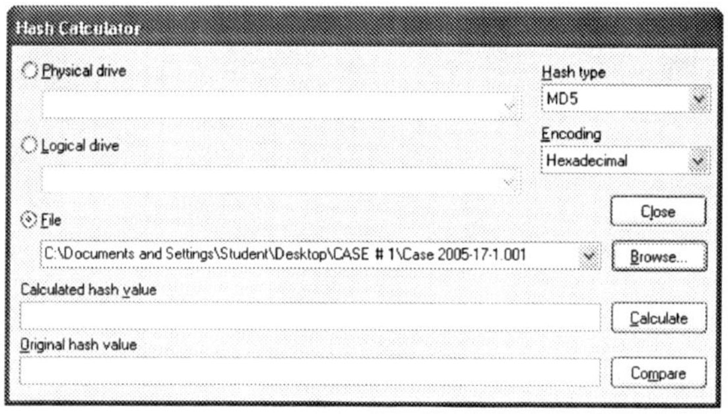

Figure 177

Click Calculate and the hash value for the image file will begin to be calculated. The hashing process will be initiated. (Figure 178)

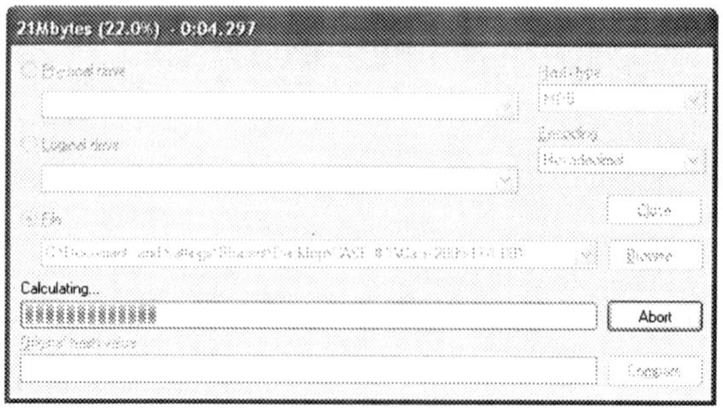

Figure 178

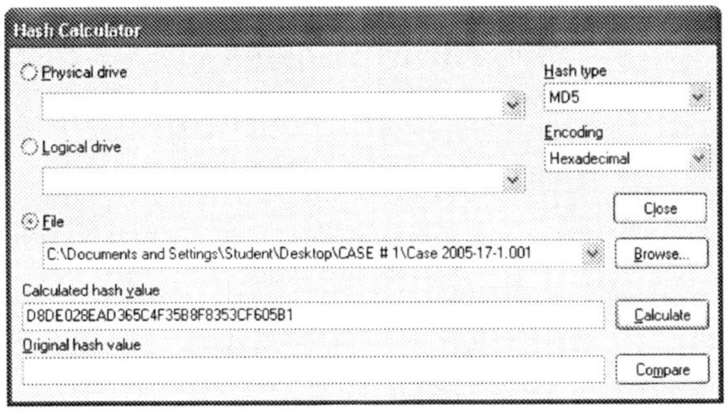

Figure 179

Once completed the hash value will be presented. Record this value.

Compare all three hash values. They should all be the same.

WinHex Hash Calculation

Figure 180

Fastream Hash Calculation

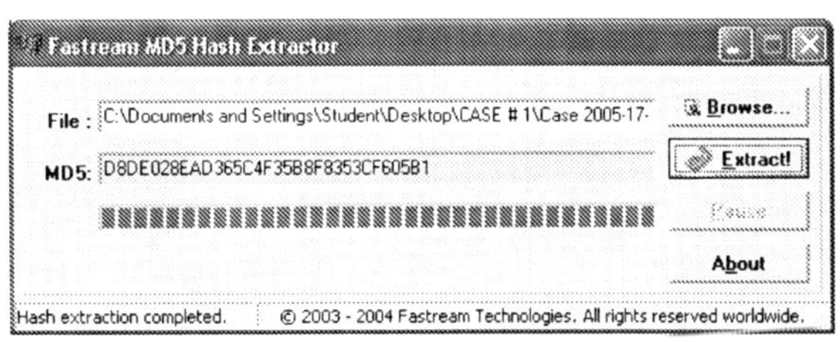

Figure 181

AccuHash Hash Calculation

Figure 182

Perform Forensics Lab # 25

TITLE: Hashing

OBJECTIVE:

To understand the concept and importance of Hashing an image, a file or data stream.

Perform Forensics Lab # 26

TITLE: Comparing the Hash for Cross Correlation

OBJECTIVE:

You may need to demonstrate the integrity of your choice of forensics tools. One method to do this is to provide a correlation between the hash of a file by two different tools. This exercise demonstrates that principle.

Steganogaphy

Steganography is the art and technique of hiding information in plain sight. With computer systems, steganography software hides various types of information or files inside of another file, including;

- Text files
- Messages
- Pictures
- Other types of files

The concept behind these types of tools is that a carrier file is that file which will contain the hidden message. This file may be a picture or some other text file. The text may be either embedded directly into the image file as individual words or sentences, or as a separate text file embedded into the carrier file.

Computer forensics examiners must be aware of steganography tools. One such popular tool is the SG.EXE application. Download this application from the web site www.download3k.com/Install-Steganography.html.

Once downloaded, click on the sg.exe icon. (Figure 183).

Figure 183

The following window should appear (Figure 184).

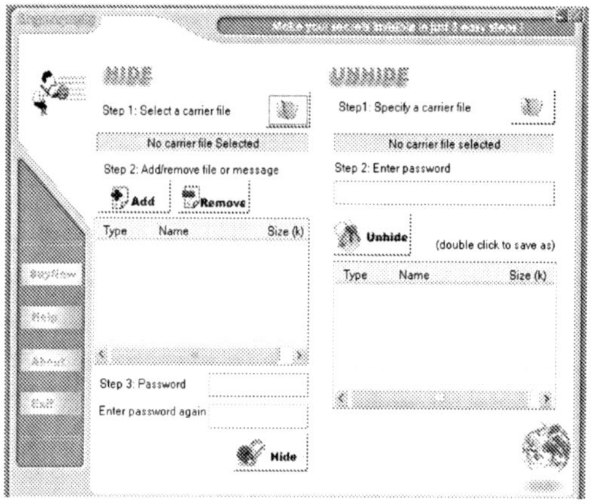

Figure 184

From this point the examiner can see how easy it is to select the carrier file by browsing to it and how to embed text information for concealment. Spend a few moments and become familiar with this program and then go to forensics lab # 27.

Perform Forensics Lab # 27

TITLE: Steganography

OBJECTIVE:

To demonstrate how to use the Steganography Version 1.50 program for the hiding and recovering of files into digital pictures.

Certifications in Computer Forensics

While some industry certifications in various technology fields are highly desirable, some have little impact in identifying highly technical or specialized skills. And as the field of computer and digital forensics evolves, eventually the effectiveness of these certifications will become more apparent.

Certifications for computer examiners is not limited to computer forensics. This is a profession that interacts with multiple other professions and disciplines. A computer forensic examiner with several technical certifications as well as some business certifications or credentials may be as marketable as one with a different set of credentials. In either respect, some base skills are required for success in this field. These skills involve computer hardware, software, applications, networking and software development.

It would be beneficial, but not required, that a computer forensic examiner have skill levels that include the CompTIA A+ level of skills, the MCSA or MCSE levels of operating systems and networking, as well as perhaps some other networking skills such as Cisco. A corporate computer examiner may utilize skills in each of these areas at various points. Some forensic examiner positions are much more focused and require less breadth of skill sets. Regardless, here are some of the industry recognized certifications in this profession.

- International Society of Forensic Computer Examiners
  CCE: Certified Computer Examiner

- International Information Systems Forensic Investigator
  CIFI: Certified Information Forensics Investigator

- Oregon State University in association with NTI
  Professional Development Certificate in Computer Forensics

Perform Forensics Lab # 28

TITLE: Computer Forensics and Computer Examiner Certifications

OBJECTIVE:

To become more familiar with the industry certifications in the profession of computer forensics.

Additional Steps in Securing the Forensics Work Environment

As has already been presented, the forensic examiner must maintain software tools, hardware tools, detailed reporting and documentation. In addition to these components, the examiner must be accurate in their time reporting. Being that cyber space covers all of earths time zones, and each connectable point within cyber space is only a mouse click away, and the variance between a wall clock, the computer time and the examiners wrist watch, a common time reference should be maintained. This section emphasises the idea of NIST Time Servers.

NIST is an acronym for National Institute for Standards and Technology. It is a common reference for various standards that is recognized by most. One component provided by NIST is that of time correlation for computer systems and networks. This involves only the downloading and installation of the nistime-32bit.exe application.

Once downloaded the examiner initialized the application by clicking on the nisttime-32bit.exe icon. (Figure 185)

Figure 185

The NISTIME 32 application will then report current system settings.

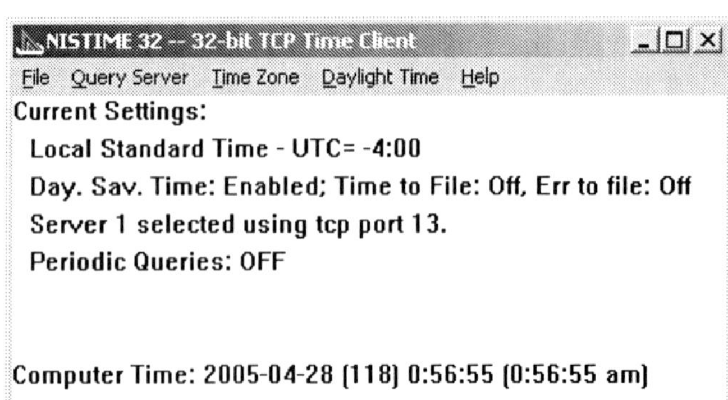

Figure 186

At this point the examiner would select the appropriate Time Server for their time zone and click OK. (Figure 187) This will be a common time reference point for the examiners system and should minimize any misunderstandings between the various time zones and standard and daylight saving time changes.

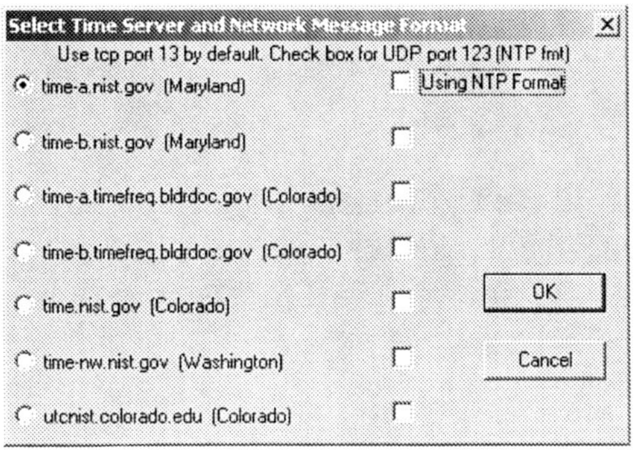

Figure 187

Your system should be synchronized with the selected time server.

Perform Forensics Lab # 29

TITLE: Configuring Windows 2000 and Windows XP to use NIST Time Servers

OBJECTIVE:

To understand the significance of accurate time reporting when dealing with systems that connect to other systems in different time zones. To rely on a recognized time standard for accuracy instead of variance in individual clocks and watches.

Computer Forensic Reporting

The importance of the forensic examination report was explained previously. This section will demonstrate one example of how to report findings. The computer examiner must develop the skill and detail in reporting their findings to their clients. The computer examiner must be able to effectively communicate their findings to both technical personnel and those who may be technologically impaired. A forensics report is the documented deliverable for the examination and must:

- Be accurate
- Be professional
- Be presented in a way that computer forensic examiners can understand
- Be presented in a way that non-computer forensic examiners can understand

In most cases, the forensic examination report must be excruciatingly detailed. A detailed example of a computer examination report is provided in the accompanying laboratory and exercise manual. The computer examiner must be able to competently describe the evidence in the case, the details of the drive image, how the integrity of the evidence was maintained, the steps performed that verified the forensic image was created accurately, be able to explain how to verify that the forensic image is an exact duplicate, how the target media was prepared and verify how the examiner did not contaminate the media during handling, acquisition, storage or analysis.

When reporting their findings, to demonstrate confidence in their work the examiner should state the exact software used to perform the examination, identify who the software is licensed to and be able to explain what the software is designed to do. Additionally, technical terminology might be better addressed with a Definitions section provided as an appendix to the report. Terms such as RAM slack, swap file, unallocated space, etc, may be common vocabulary to another examiner but it may also be foreign to a non-forensic examiner.

The report must be written in a logical sequence. Simply saying that you acquired some evidence and secured it is inadequate. The examiner needs to be able to explain that the evidence drive was removed from a secure storage location for analysis and when it was returned.

Conclusions and opinions:

- All conclusions or opinions must be founded upon sound forensic principals. Theories must be tested and documented with the outcome. Example, if a disk was formatted, explain why you know it was formatted.

- If the report is to be continuous, cut and paste the relevant documents into the report body. If you do not want to make the report continuous then include any recovered files or documents as an attachment and include a reference such as "see exhibit #."

- Document the chain of custody for each piece of evidence and provide the documentation in your report.

- Document the disposition of all evidence.

- Convert all evidence to a viewable and presentable format.

- If the operating system uses the FAT filesystem, examine the File Allocation Table with an acceptable hex editor.

- You are not to make judgments of the evidence. Your responsibility is that of the examiner.

- Do not say that you destroyed any handwritten notes you made.

- Include any and all passwords you find in your report.

Case Reporting Example

This section presents an example of the forensics case report.

Computer Forensic Examination
Case 1/11/05-001
Date
January 11, 2005

Investigator
D. B. Cooper
CISSP, CCE, A+

This document is for internal use only.
All information contained within is
considered strictly confidential.

Page 1 of 35

A case report should contain a minimum of the following:

REPORT INDEX

FTK Report Wizard

FTK provides a report wizard option for each case. This provides an electronic copy of FTK actions, discoveries and examiner comments. Additionally, the printed or text case report may be imported into the report wizard. To initialize the report wizard:

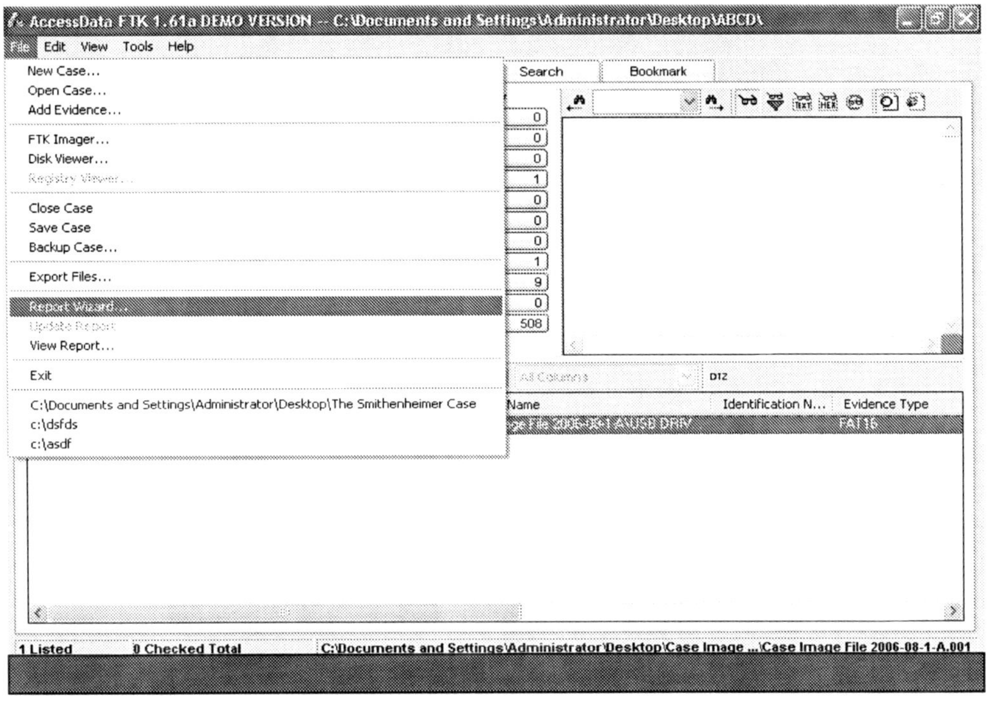

Figure 188

Select File and chose Report Wizard from the drop down window.

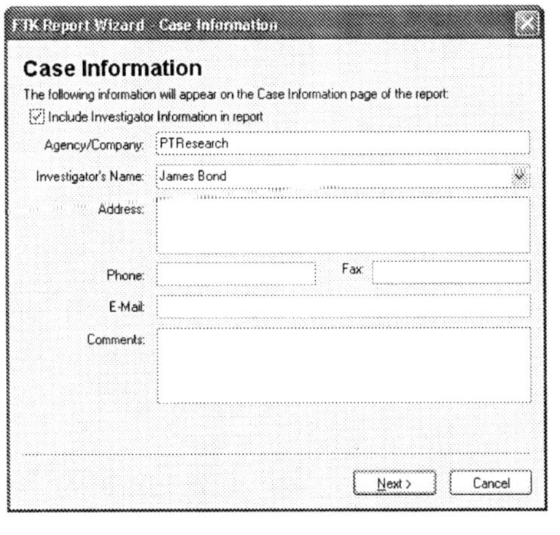

Figure 189

Complete the Case Information. This is a very important step in forensic reporting as it identifies who worked on the case and is included in the report.

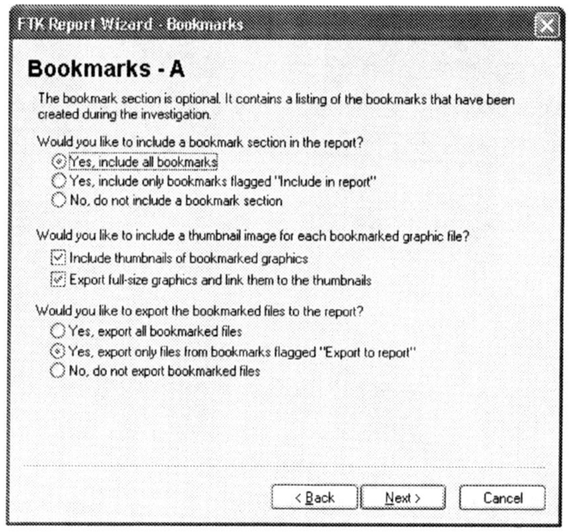

Figure 190

The next step is to identify which bookmarks are to be included in the report. Bookmarks are examiner selections of specific or unique files that are of interest to the case. These files may include discovered photos or pictures, text information or some other items.

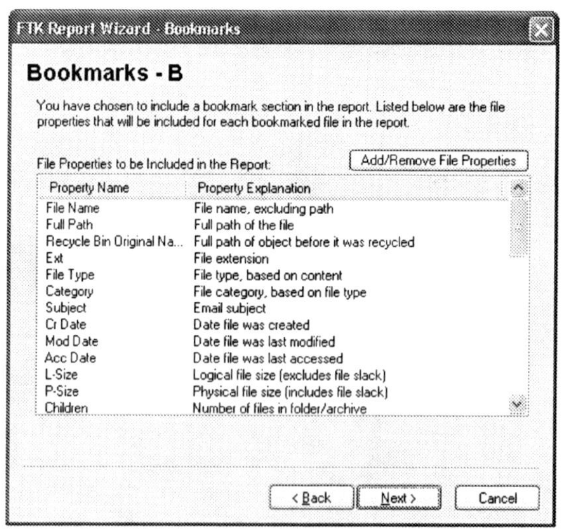

Figure 191

Once the examiner clicks the Next button the File Properties Bookmarks window will appear. This step identifies which file properties will be noted for each file. Again, this is a very important step and identifies the file size, location in the media, and last accessed and modified dates. One significant factor of this is that this information demonstrates the frozen state of the disk and how the files have not been altered by the operating system during examination.

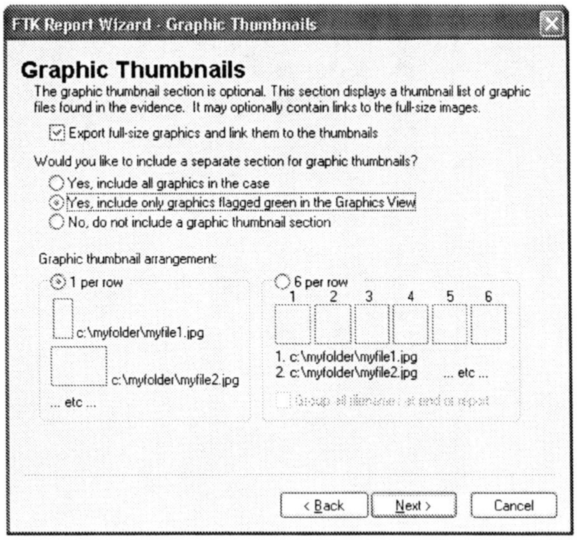

Figure 192

The next report wizard window to appear allows the examiner to select graphic thumbnails for inclusion into the report. This option will provide the recipient of the report a point and click approach to viewing all of the identified graphic files in a thumbnail formation. Select the defaults and click Next.

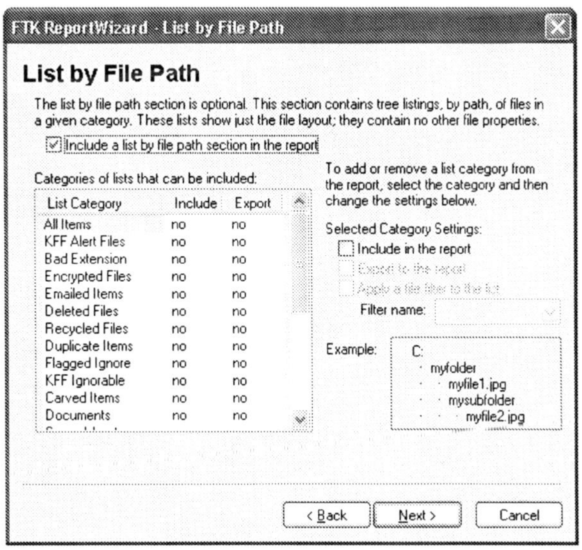

Figure 193

The List by File Path window is presented next. This window permits the examiner to include file path tree listings of files. Select the Include a list by file path section in the report and click Next.

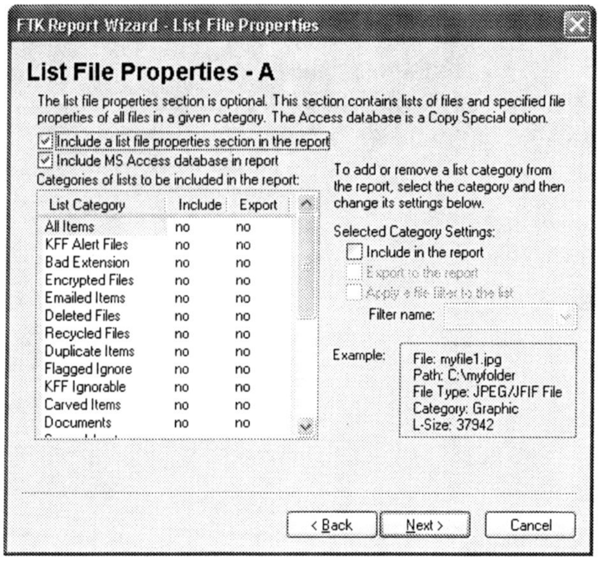

Figure 194

Where the previous window provided the option to list files by path, this window permits selection of a file list by properties. Combined, these two windows identifies the specifics about where a file is located in the media and its individual parameters. Select the Include a list file properties section in the report and click Next.

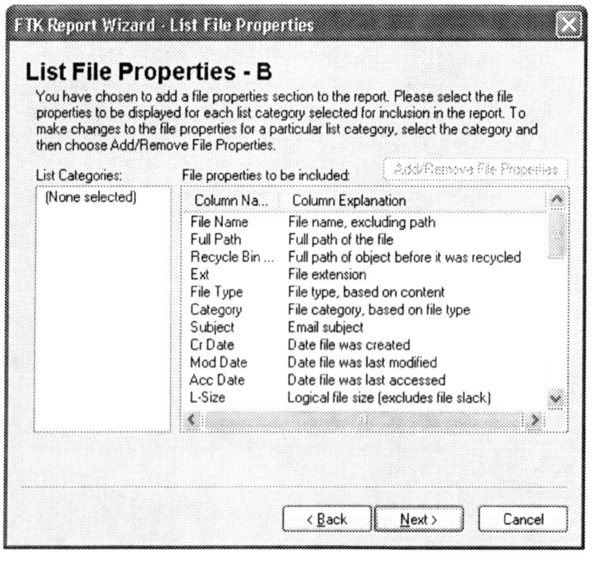

Figure 195

A window that confirms the examiners selections will appear. If the desired settings are selected, click Next. Otherwise, click Back to make any changes.

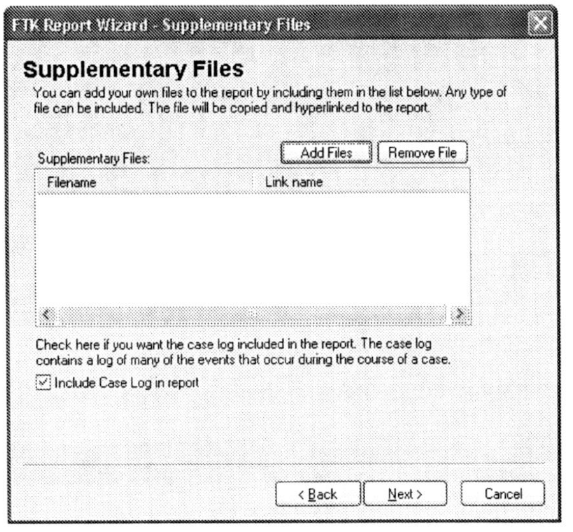

Figure 196

At this point FTK provides the option of importing any other text files that may be associated with this case. These files may include the Chain-of-Custody form, Evidence Handling Procedures, Receipt of Equipment, or the written examiner report as identified in the laboratory procedures manual. Make your selections and click Next.

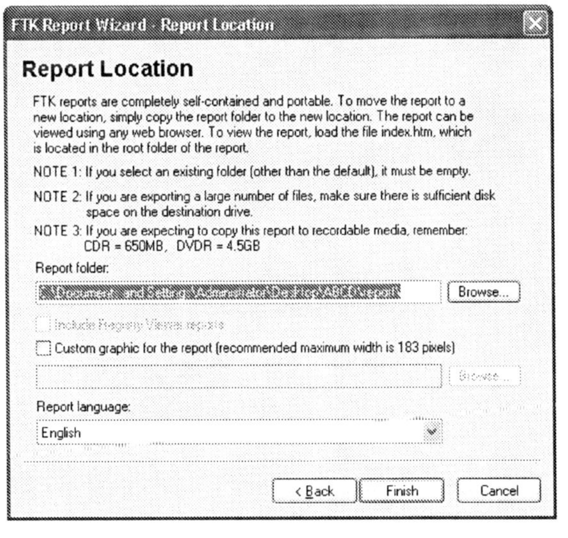

Figure 197

The Report Location window appears and is where the location of where the report is to be stored is selected. Computer examiners should maintain an organized and efficient system for naming and storing reports so as to not confuse them with reports from other cases. Select a location and click Finish.

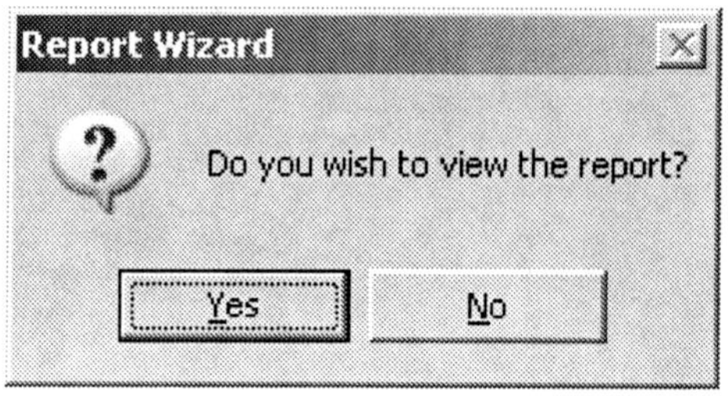

Figure 198

The option to view the report is presented. Click Yes.

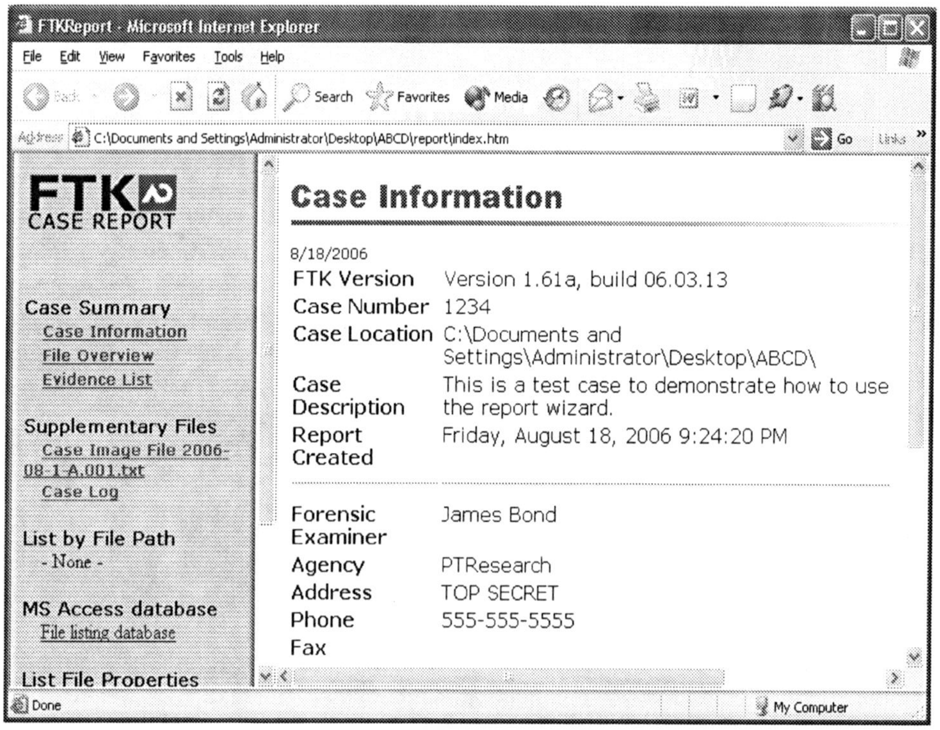

Figure 199

The report is presented to the examiner. Note the file selection options in the left column.

Chain of Custody Documentation

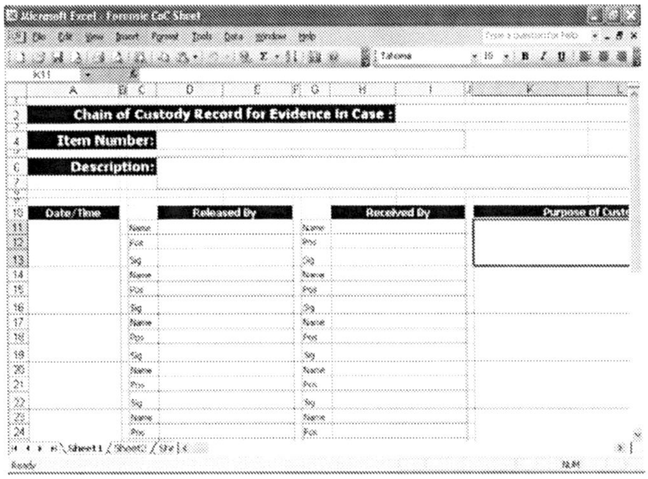

Figure 200

Whether it is the corporate environment or in law enforcement, chain of custody documentation is vital to maintaining consistency in handling and reporting and for demonstrating proper security of an evidence drive. The examiner should create a Chain-of-Custody form for their organization. Chain of Custody documentation must be maintained and should accompany any forensic recovery. Image files, original media or any other information is not to be disclosed to any third party unless required by law.

Evidence Handling Policy

Each computer examiner and organization that provides forensic services should have a documented evidence handling policy. This is to prevent cross contamination between cases and prior to use in any analysis or recovery, the working drive must be forensically sterile. This may be accomplished by performing a full reformat and includes virus protection software for all associated systems. The working drive is the drive used to store the target image and will have no other images or files stored on it. After completion of each case, acquired image files may be stored on an alternate data base system or the image drive may be stored in a secure location.

The evidence handling policy should dictate that the storage of original media must be consistent with local law enforcement procedures with original media to be stored in a storage safe and protected from fire, water and environmental concerns. Additionally, all stored original media must be labelled by forensic case number

Perform Forensics Lab # 30

TITLE: Create a Report Using FTK Report Wizard

OBJECTIVE:

1. To become familiar with how to create a report that is presentable to a client for services rendered.

2. Use the FTK Report Wizard for reporting your analyses and findings.

Perform Forensics Lab # 31

TITLE: Reporting your Findings; Writing Reports and Documentation

OBJECTIVE:

To guide the learner towards the ability to adequately present findings from a forensics evaluation.

Interviewing and Being Interviewed

It is important to understand that as corporate computer examiners, you are not law enforcement. Too many times the response from college students to the question of "What do you do in this case?, or What do you do in this circumstance?" yields a response of "I would get a search warrant". The role of the corporate examiner is to work with law enforcement and be consistent and equitable in your dealings with all employees. You need to know when to contact law enforcement and when not to. You should remember that you may or may not interview individuals regarding forensic images or computer use. Additionally, you should take notes and have another employee with you during any situation where you may believe the finding may result in legal involvement.

Law enforcement personnel are trained in interviewing and interrogation. You as a corporate examiner most likely are not. Law enforcement frequently are exposed to something known as the Reid Technique ® which consists of three components:

1. Factual Analysis

2. Interviewing

3. Interrogation

It takes training and practice to become proficient in this technique but this is not the focus of this training. However, you can benefit significantly and receive greater insight by performing labs # 32, Being Interviewed in a Forensics Investigation, and lab # 33, Conducting a Personal Interview in a Forensics Investigation

Perform Forensics Lab # 32

TITLE: Being Interviewed in a Forensics Investigation

OBJECTIVE:

To become familiar with the interview process with the opportunity to meet with a law enforcement official to learn how they conduct interviews, the types of interviews and how they process and report the results.

Perform Forensics Lab # 33

TITLE: Conducting a Personal Interview in a Forensics Investigation

OBJECTIVE:

To become familiar with the interview process with the opportunity to conduct a mock interview.

Perform Forensics Lab # 34

TITLE: Evidence Handling Policy

OBJECTIVE:

To become familiar with an example of an Evidence Handling Policy.

Perform Forensics Lab # 35

TITLE: Chain of Custody

OBJECTIVE:

To become accustomed to documenting secure handling, processing, storage and transportation of devices in order to demonstrate integrity in handling.

Perform Forensics Lab # 36

TITLE: Creating a Receipt

OBJECTIVE:

To understand the importance of creating a documented the receiving or providing of evidence.

Perform Forensics Lab # 37

TITLE: Analyze Case Image file 2005-40

OBJECTIVE:

To analyze a particular media to determine if any information of evidentiary value is contained within and to report on it.

Legal Terms and Definitions

Being familiar with legal terms and definitions is an important aspect of the computer forensics field. Many people do not know the difference between different types of laws. In the U.S. there is civil law, criminal law and administrative law.

Civil law pertains to non-criminal law and is the basis for most state legal systems. A dispute between land owners may typically fall under civil law. Criminal law pertains to those legal statutes where crimes against the public apply. This may include subjects such as robbery, extortion and assault. Administrative law involves regulatory issues and legal restrictions and may involve fines to those who violate these regulatory issues. The examiner may wish to reference Blacks Law Dictionary and / or Law.com for definitions, examples or explanations to many legal terms. Each of the following terms are included in the laboratory procedure and should be researched. The accompanying laboratory procedure provides this exercise.

Accessory	Accomplice	Attorney-Client Privilege
Arraignment	Arrest Warrant	Burden of Proof
Confession	Complaint	Competent Evidence
Consent	Court Order	Crime
Criminal Law	Cross Examination	Cybersquatting
Damages	Decree	Defamation
Defendant	Disclosure	Discovery
Eavesdropping	Electronic Signature	Embezzlement
Entrapment	Espionage	Evidence
Evidence Handling	Exculpatory	Exhibit
Expert	Felony	Force Majeure
Forgery	Fraud	FOIA
Frivolous Suit	Fruit of the Poisonous Tree	
Habeas Corpus	Harassment	Harm

Hearing	Hearsay	Hyperlink
Inadmissible	Incompetence	Inculpatory
Indemnify	Independent Contractor	
Informed consent	Infringment	Inside Information
Intangible	Intellectual Property	Intent
Joint Venture	Judgement	Jurisdiction
Knock and Announce		Lewd
Liability	Liable	Libel
Lis Pendens	Malfeasance	Malice
Malpractice	Mediation	Minor
Miranda Warning	Misdemeanor	Misrepresentation
Mitigate	Negligence	Nominal Damages
Non-Competition Agreement		Non-Disclosure Agreement
Oath	OSHA	Offer
Order	Pain and Suffering	Paralegal
Patent	Plagiarism	Plaintiff
Power of Attorney	Precedent	Presumption of Innocence
Preliminary Injunction		Pro Se
Property	Prosecute	Public Domain
Punitive Damages	Quantum Meruit	Quitclaim
Reasonable Doubt	Red Herring	Reformation
Retainer	Search Warrant	Sexual Harassment
Slander	Small Claims Court	Spam

Statute Statute of Limitations Subpoena

Summons Testify Theft

Spam Statute Statute of Limitations

Subpoena Summons Testify

Theft Uniform Resource Locator

Unjust Enrichment Warrant Warranty

With Prejudice Witness Work for Hire.

Perform Forensics Lab # 38

TITLE: Legal Terms and Definitions

OBJECTIVE:

To have the learner become familiar with common legal terms associated with computer forensics and identify if the topic falls under civil, criminal, regulatory law, or other.

Additional Documentation for Forensic Handling

U.S. Government guildines on handling and processing of electronic evidence is based upon years of involvement with electronic crime scenes. The importance of a sanitary environment when processing, handling and acquiring electronic storage media is vital to the legal processing and prosecution of criminal cases. For the corporate computer examiner it is also vital that these precautions be adhered to for turning over the discovery of suspected criminal activity to law enforcement.

This section introduces additional information regarding legal issues and guides for possible crime scene handling. The docuementation is provided by the U.S. Department of Justice. These resources can be obtained at http://www.ncjrs.org/pdffiles1/nij/187736.pdf and http://www.ncjrs.org/pdffiles1/nij/199408.pdf.

Forensics lab # 39 provides an extensive assignment regarding these publications.

Perform Forensics Lab # 39

TITLE: United States Department of Justice, Electronic Crime Scene Investigation Guide for First Responders

OBJECTIVE:

To introduce the learner to the environment, steps and thought process of law enforcement dealing with electronic crime scenes.

Perform Forensics Lab # 40

TITLE: United States Department of Justice, Forensic Examination of Digital Evidence: A Guide for Law Enforcement.

OBJECTIVE:

To introduce the learner to the environment, steps and thought process of law enforcement computer forensic examiners. The steps identified in this procedure follow recommended guidelines for electronic crime scene first responders.

Case Scenario for Case Image File 2005-45

You work for the county and you have been called to the local library where one of the librarians was concerned about a suspicious looking individual using the computer. The librarian stated she wanted the computer "looked at" for any thing suspicious as the patron kept closing the browser anytime she would come near the computer. The librarian stated that after the suspicious acting patron left the premises, she brought up the browser and tried to see where he had been but all history had been deleted.

You arrived at the library 8:05 AM the next morning and discovered the computer in question in a powered off state. You removed the drive from the computer and placed it into a secure container and left a note on the computer that it was out of service. You provided the librarian with a receipt and began a chain-of-custody form. The name of the librarian is Linda Johansen.

Perform Forensics Lab # 41

TITLE: Analyze Case Image file 2005-45

OBJECTIVE:

To analyze a particular media to determine if any information of evidentiary value is contained within and to report on it.

Write a Case Image Report for this case and include:

- Cover Page
- Table of Contents
- Chain-of-Custody
- Receipt
- Summary of Case
- Listing of All Evidence Items
- Case Summary
- Case Log Information
- Any pertinent pictures or images
- Any pertinent documents or files
- Any Applicable Policy References

Perform Forensics Lab # 42

TITLE: Analyze Case Image File 2006-50

OBJECTIVE:

To perform a forensic analysis on a computer media. You are to treat this exercise as a real case, taking all precautions and documenting all steps in accordance with recognized forensics investigation and reporting.

Errata Sheet

For any errors in this manual, please send an e-mail to

info@cyberdefenseresearch.com

In the subject line put: **Errata Sheet for Computer Forensics I**

You can then enter the following information in the body of the e-mail:

Describe error:

Page/s where error is located:

Printed in the United States
217982BV00001B/37/A